friends —
With Love,
Patti

A
Vision
Fulfilled

A
Vision
Fulfilled

Patti Penny's Journey

MICHAEL PULLEY

ARCHWAY
PUBLISHING

Archway Publishing books may be ordered through booksellers or by contacting:

Archway Publishing
1663 Liberty Drive
Bloomington, IN 47403
www.archwaypublishing.com
1 (888) 242-5904

ISBN: 978-1-4808-8662-9 (sc)
ISBN: 978-1-4808-8661-2 (hc)
ISBN: 978-1-4808-8663-6 (e)

Library of Congress Control Number: 2020903905

Print information available on the last page.

Archway Publishing rev. date: 04/14/2020

To Jeani Thomson, copy editor extraordinaire

Acknowledgments

MY DEEPEST THANKS TO PATTI Penny for her patience during all the hours, days, weeks, and months we talked and wrote to each other, collecting information about her life and work, and thanks for her openness and honesty throughout the process. I am especially appreciative and amazed at her ever-present insights and memory.

Thanks to Al Penny who through his quiet and stalwart strength backed and encouraged Patti through this book process and throughout their marriage and Patti's career.

Thanks to the following who agreed to interviews, providing valuable background and data: daughter Paula Adams, president at Penmac; Sharon Triplett Cotton, childhood/current friend; Carol Hutchinson Scott, teenage/current friend; Phyllis Rotrock, long-time friend of Patti's; John Sellars, executive director of History Museum on the Square in Springfield, Missouri; Helen Lamb, curator of the Seymour, Missouri History Museum; Dolores Matney, Seymour, Missouri, historian; Tim Massey, Penmac CEO; Leah Ann Iaguessa, Penmac CFO; and Sara Corman, Penmac marketing director. And thanks to Mason Duchatschek, speechwriter.

Special thanks to Geoffrey Stewart and Morgan Judy at Archway Publishing for shepherding this project so thoughtfully, kindly, and professionally through its many stages.

Many thanks to Jeani Thomson for her encouragement and keen editorial eye.

Contents

Foreword

PATTI PENNY FOUND MY EMAIL address at the bottom of a newspaper column and wrote a polite message: "Several people have asked me to write a book about my life experiences. I do not have the ability to complete such a project. In fact, I do not know where to start."

After spending a large part of my life writing novels, short stories, a memoir, and newspaper columns, I understood her at once because I usually never knew where to start either. Writing for me has always been a struggle.

"Would it be possible that you could take on such a project?"

What exactly did she want? An overblown pamphlet to bolster her ego? I didn't know this woman other than a shadowy memory of hearing her name mentioned around town from time to time.

I was retired and finally doing my own full-time writing, content writing bi-weekly newspaper columns, delving into my past, and attempting to merge it with something relevant for today's reader. At last, I was devoting several uninterrupted hours a day to fiction writing, hoping to add stories to a collection of pieces published in literary journals over the years. Maybe I would write another novel. In short, I lived the long-awaited life of writing and reading.

She went on, "I would be very grateful for your consideration." That boilerplate request was businesslike enough to be ignored out of hand. Then the final sentence: "I love your style of writing."

Does a writer exist who could dismiss that sentence? It didn't read, "I love your writing" or "You're a good writer." Nothing significant embedded in those empty declarations. But "style of writing." She acknowledged what most writers strive for—a unique touch that might impact a reader. She had my attention. Worth a reply. We would meet.

Her company, Penmac, was in downtown Springfield, Missouri. I had been by it many times. I was greeted by a receptionist who appeared to know why I was there and told me to have a seat at a small round table by the door. I purposely arrived fifteen minutes early to observe what kind of place this was.

"Would you like some coffee?"

"No, thank you."

The receptionist handled many tasks with ease: typing on a computer, speaking with people entering, taking phone calls. People (apparently Penmac employees) walked in and out of offices along a long narrow hallway, all cordially greeting the receptionist. A stack of League of Women Voters brochures—a voters' guide for an upcoming election—sat on the table. Two of the arriving people sat with me and filled out forms the receptionist gave them.

Hanging up the phone, the receptionist said, "Patti apologizes that she will be about ten minutes late from an earlier appointment. She is very sorry."

Busy woman. I still had not decided if I wanted to take on such a project. I knew nothing about running a business or about writing someone's life story. If this woman wanted me to write a glowing homage to her fine self, then I would cordially decline on the grounds of being too busy or some such excuse. I would not spend endless hours writing at the behest of some egoist. That, I knew. Nothing lost, nothing gained.

I sensed the woman walking in was not a client, customer, or employee coming in late for work. She looked directly at me and said, "You must be Michael, and I can't tell you how sorry I am to keep you waiting. I usually don't do this." Her handshake was firm, eyes directly on me, a slight frown befitting her apology. Then, as if she were ten minutes early, she smiled and said we could go to a conference room. Apologies made, she was now ready to talk.

The upstairs room was small. A table contained miscellaneous papers, which she whisked to one side before she walked to a coffee maker, and not finding coffee there, said, "Well, I guess we can do without that."

She wore a blouse that matched a vest-like garment—tasteful, not ostentatious—and I knew it was not from Walmart. She explained she had been at the Maple Park Cemetery Board meeting discussing how to raise money for the old iron fence surrounding the property. "It's a beautiful place and needs to be kept up."

I agreed. It was just a few blocks from downtown.

"Now," she said, "I've always liked your columns. We may have had similar childhoods. Small town and all." Her small town was Seymour, Missouri, and before I could start taking notes, she began telling me about the town, her childhood, her grandparents, her friends, and her high school days.

I asked what kind of book she wanted.

She was not sure.

Did she want one about her life or her business?

She hesitated, unsure. Then she asked what I thought was a curious question: "What kind of book do you think it should be?"

That's when I knew we were partners—I not necessarily the hired hand, she not necessarily the overriding boss.

I asked, "Who do you see as your readers?"

Another long pause. "I hadn't thought about that much."

Apparently, she sincerely wanted my input.

I later learned through my own research that this kind, unassuming woman sitting in a small, cluttered conference room had begun a business in 1988, which currently operates thirty-two offices in nine states; had received numerous kudos, including an honorary doctorate from Missouri State University; awarded a Springfieldian of the Year Award from the chamber of commerce; served on many community volunteer boards; elected to the Springfield Public Schools Board of Education; had given numerous speeches to civic and humanitarian organizations; and received the prestigious Missourian Award.

I left our first hour-long meeting still mostly undecided, but I promised her I would soon make a decision. Within a week, I submitted a three-page proposal, with a possible structure to the forthcoming book, timelines, fee. She accepted. And we launched a partnership. I was honored to be part of it.

In these pages, I hope to capture much of her personal history—fears, setbacks, regrets, and successes—and how her pre-business experiences shaped her, forming her into a caring, hardworking woman who is unafraid of taking chances and always treats people fairly. Her story is about the struggles inherent in achieving the American dream, which has guided so many for so long.

Michael Pulley
2019

1

Isolation

IN 1941, A YOUNG GIRL in Seymour, Missouri, was within eleven days of celebrating her first birthday when, on December 7, the Imperial Japanese Navy Air Service flew two separate waves of attackers into Pearl Harbor, Hawaii, sending the United States into World War II in both the Pacific and European theaters. Patti Halbert, an avid reader by age ten, would later learn that 2,335 American servicemen died and 1,143 were wounded, with eighteen ships sunk or run aground in Pearl Harbor. Several naval ships harbored there were destroyed, such as the *Nevada, Arizona, West Virginia, California, Utah, Oklahoma,* and *Maryland.* She learned that in books. But before she could read, she would also learn from her mother and grandmother that her mother's brother, Uncle Sam (a fitting name), enlisted in the US Army Air Corps at age eighteen and flew an A-20-A bomber in the Third Attack Group in the Pacific. And her step-grandfather, Ed Anderson, went to Ft. Chaffee, Arkansas, as a hospital medic. Most men of Seymour were away at the war. As the adult Patti

(Halbert) Penny said later, "My early life had very little male influence."

Did such a seminal event in US history influence the young girl directly, as it did almost every citizen at the time? Indeed. Some of her first memories were of food rationing. For example, her mother went on a date (Patti never knew her father) to Half a Hill dance hall in Springfield, Missouri, and stole a sugar dispenser. The daughter, being so young, thought it was wrong but was amused her mother would do such a thing.

Much of her childhood was happy. During the war, her mother opened a beauty shop on the town square to make money. Women in town and on farms were receiving military checks sent from their husbands away at war. Also, the women began working at a tomato-canning plant that shipped the processed product overseas to servicemen. Thus, many women had income for such things as permanents and manicures. The business prospered.

Patti, her mother, and her grandmother lived above the shop until the war ended, and then moved behind the shop and rented the upstairs to a returning war veteran and his German bride. During the war, the talk of the town revolved around hostility toward the Japanese and Germans. So when trying to assimilate his bride into Seymour culture, the veteran was often met with stern silences, if not open rebuke. Patti's mother, Mary, never harbored resentment toward the German bride, Sylvia, thinking such discrimination was wrong, but mostly because Sylvia was also a hairdresser.

Patti wondered why her mother would allow the enemy in the upstairs apartment. "I hate her," she told her mother.

"Patti, you shouldn't feel that way!"

That did not stop the sassy girl from berating Sylvia whenever she could.

Years later, the older Patti said, "I said some pretty mean

things to her, which I've always regretted." The couple left not long after moving in. Mary blamed Patti, causing a rift, among many others, between mother and daughter.

Still, Patti was mostly content living above the beauty shop. Her strong-willed mother (years later, Patti's daughter, Paula, called her "not kind") never backed down from asserting herself to Patti and anyone else in town. Mary spied a tricycle she did not have enough money to buy and, by flattery or through sheer scam, convinced the owner to give the tricycle to Patti. Patti never knew the exact nature of the transaction, but she was certain her mother conned the owner into relinquishing the child's vehicle.

The tricycle gave Patti the means to leave the isolation of her upstairs apartment as she pedaled around the Seymour square. Because she was not big enough to ride a bicycle, many wondered if the small girl should have the unfettered freedom not usually allowed someone her age: four and five years old. However, neither Patti nor her mother listened to any whispers from locals who were not accustomed to such a free-spirited little girl and the forthright mother, who from her stern demeanor made plain she would not tolerate an argument from anyone daring to step in her way.

The shop was always busy while Patti often lay on her stomach with her coloring book, pretending not to listen but hearing all manner of town gossip laid out in the tones and cadences of Ozarkian speech. Patti's grandmother did the shampooing and cleaning, and Mary cut hair, gave manicures, and applied permanents; women wanted their perms in tight curls so they would last.

Perhaps Mary's salon was popular because of a permanent wave machine she purchased at great price, and it had paid for itself in a short time. The machine had many metal clamps dangling from wires. After twisting the hair onto rollers, she would affix them onto the clamps and turn on the heat. The hair dryers were loud enough so that plenty of gossip was directed toward the silent women trapped under the machines, none the wiser that they were being discussed—often with rancor. Patti caught everything, her first encounter with how business involved people—sometimes at their best and sometimes not—carrying on at various levels while providing a service and hoping for a profit.

The beauty shop business offered Patti a certain security, giving her the freedom to roam around town and the opportunity to make friends, such as Janice Cawthra, whose grandparents owned the Owen Movie Theater. They spent most Saturday afternoons being entertained by typical 1940s movie house fare: newsreels of national and world events, a must for anyone in Seymour wanting to see footage of how the war in Europe and the Pacific was taking place; several cartoons; and previews of coming attractions. Patti and Janice loved westerns featuring Roy Rogers and other stars. And to round out their adventures, they rode Janice's horse, Dot. Janice sat in the saddle with Patti behind and wrapped her arms around her friend's midsection, trying not to fall, while Janice put Dot through her paces. Patti bounced precariously behind. They often imagined scenes from the westerns they had recently seen: two young girls atop Dot as the horse trotted and often galloped through pastures. It was a nearly idyllic adventure for two childhood friends.

In the sixth grade, Patti quickly learned the jolt and pain of separation when Janice moved to California. In later years, Patti said, "Janice's leaving broke my heart." She saw Janice again at age fifteen when she returned to Seymour to visit her grandparents. Their reunion was short yet joyous. When Patti told her goodbye, neither knew they would never see each other again. Word reached Patti in the late 1980s that Janice had died of a drug overdose.

Randall Tate was another childhood friend. His grandparents

owned Lowery Grocery Store, where he and Patti were allowed all the Grapette and Orangette sodas they wanted. They often drank them under a tree behind the store while eating bologna sandwiches. They could climb into a tree house that was equipped with all the amenities two kids might want in their private getaway: a rug, wooden benches, and an electric light powered by a line running to the grocery store. Randall was a year older than Patti. When he entered first grade, leaving her behind, a social rift developed that was never bridged. In her adult years, Patti heard Randall had been in and out of trouble with the law.

Both childhood friends left Patti—one to California and one through social separation—alone to feel the emotional isolation of loss. Later, as an adult, she appreciated her eventual good fortune through hard work and sheer gumption, leading to a fulfilling life. She recalled the pleasant adventures with those friends and sadness with their leaving.

One of Patti's earliest memories was of Mary Nell White's wedding, to which she was not invited. From an upstairs window, Patti watched the rain falling steadily and flowing down the street. Her grandmother, seeing her there, said, "If it rains on your wedding day, you will shed a tear for every raindrop." Mary Nell's husband, Dave, was from Minnesota and never assimilated into Seymour. For a time, he helped run Mary Nell's family business, but he never felt accepted. After the store closed, the couple moved to Springfield.

When Patti turned five, her mother decided Patti should attend church. She bought her a new dress, but even though Patti admired the dress, she refused to go. Arms crossed, she looked directly at her mother and said, "I will not go." But her mother could be as insistent as her daughter—and even more so. After finally getting the dress onto Patti, she took her by the hand and marched her out of the apartment and down the street to the Methodist church. As they got to the two large doors leading in—huge and forbidding to the young girl—the terrified Patti broke loose from her mother's grip and ran all the way home, vowing never to return. But a few Sundays later, Mary lured her back to the church for a pancake breakfast, Patti's favorite food. Apparently, the girl would not agree to anything without getting something in return. Perhaps the beginning of a burgeoning business sense.

One wonders if the adult Patti Penny in 1989—only one year after opening the fledgling Penmac staffing company—remembered her fear and isolation after cutting from Mary Halbert's grasp and dashing back to their apartment alone. In that second year of owning her own business, Patti had just left a comfortable and successful employment at St. John's Hospital in Springfield. In the personnel department, she had gotten a taste of hiring qualified and competent people—and leading them into meaningful and financially secure jobs. Could she have been content remaining at St. John's—maybe for the rest of her working life? Perhaps. But upon the encouragement of others, especially her husband, Al Penny, she and Jackie McKinsey launched a start-up that would occupy and sustain her for the rest of her life until retirement and would eventually expand into nine states.

Yet, Patti recalls the loneliness and isolation in 1989 when she decided the company (in this case, herself) would transport associates to their work sites as temporary employees. Penmac was supplying labor twenty-four hours a day and seven days a week to Springfield and Nixa manufacturers, but many associates were unable to take themselves to work. No Penny family members helped. Even Al, who had been entirely supportive of Patti starting the company, said, "Nobody ever took me to work, and I am not going to take anyone."

Exactly what had she gotten herself into?

"It was exhausting for me," she said years later, looking back on those trying times. In fact, nearly hopeless. Many people, including Al, thought she was not just *perhaps* doing the wrong thing but was doing *exactly* the wrong thing. In her retirement, she confided, "At the time, I remember thinking about the story of the Little Red Hen." Could she do it herself? Much remained to be seen.

Still, in 1989, she was out there alone, isolated from others, facing fears and perplexities every day. But persevering, nonetheless.

Patti's early forebears were no strangers to hard times. Seeking better conditions, they had left Kentucky, Tennessee, and North Carolina, migrating from poor settlements into south Missouri, a much-traveled migration route into the Ozarks for many hill folks. Alas, they found rugged hills similar to what they had left, just as their kin years before found in Appalachia. Prior to that, in the British Isles, many Scots had migrated into Northern Ireland, a Protestant enclave, and stayed there for a time before crossing the ocean to the United States. Because of their brief sojourn in Ireland, they were labeled Scotch-Irish, but remained Scottish, nonetheless, in custom and tradition. Unable to continue the proud Scottish tradition of making good Scotch whiskey from barley, the newly arrived US settlers soon discovered corn as a source of distilling spirits. Thus arose the Appalachian affinity for corn whiskey, perhaps not purely the makings of Scotch whiskey, but close enough for their taste.

Sam and Mary Hale Stephens boarded a train in Prestonsburg, Kentucky, with all their earthly possessions and six children. Patti's grandmother Dorcas was one of those children arriving in tiny Diggins, Missouri. Sam and Mary left their Kentucky home because the eastern part of the state had become lawless. For example, a year before they left, their oldest daughter, Nora, was killed by a rejected suitor. He had come to their home, called her name, and as she approached, shot her through the door. Also, Mary Stephen's sister's husband had murdered a man. Thus, fleeing to Missouri, they changed their name to "Hale" to avoid prosecution.

Upon his arrival at Sarvis Point, Sam Stephens sought a good cattle buyer. He met Everett Jennings who told Stephens he would help him buy good white-faced cattle, but Jennings actually wanted to meet Stephens' black-haired daughter, Dorcas. They married April 7, 1913, at the Greene County Courthouse in Springfield.

Patti's grandfather Everett Jennings was enterprising, to say the least. When his father gave him a checkbook and was instructed to buy cattle throughout south Missouri and northern Arkansas. He would drive the cattle back to Seymour on horseback and sleep in farmers' barns, keeping the cattle corralled around the barn. In the mornings, a farmer would see the cattle and say, "I see Everett's in the barn."

On his cattle-buying ventures, he left his wife, Dorcas, alone in what she called "the terrible solitude of Missouri." She told Patti she sat on the front steps of their house near Sarvis Point and listened to the plaintive moan of the whippoorwills. "My grandmother said she was so lonely, she thought she would die."

While living behind the beauty shop, her mother's boyfriend, Homer Chaffin, gave Patti a pet cocker spaniel named Pepper, whom Patti loved and played with constantly. Her mother was proud Pepper was a pedigree. When not in the house, the dog was tethered with a long leash to a clothesline extending nearly the length of the backyard. Patti came home one day to find the dog had climbed the high back porch and fallen through the steps. He hung by the leash. Today, Patti said, "That is something I will never forget." Her mother mourned the loss of the breed more than the death of Patti's pet.

The conclusion of World War II—a watershed event for the United States and the world—brought changes nationwide as the military returned home to what would surely be, at last, peaceful prosperity. And much was good. No more rationing, men greeted their families and went to work. The GI Bill allowed soldiers to enter college, foreshadowing better times, and babies boomed. "The end of the war changed my life," says Patti.

But not all in Patti's life was positive. Uncle Sam returned and stayed with Patti, her mother, and her grandmother, hoping to get his life back. According to Patti, "His beautiful black hair had turned white. He lost some of his teeth because of the filthy conditions in the Philippines. He was a nervous wreck, chain-smoking Camels and drinking black coffee." But he was able to buy a big, black Cadillac and took Patti and her mother and grandmother to the Ozark Empire Fair where Patti saw colorful rubber balloons for the first time: "the most beautiful sight I had ever seen." During the war, because of rubber rationing, such things did not exist.

In 1948, when Patti was eight years old, she, her mother, and her stepfather, Bill Boring, moved to a small farm a mile outside Seymour. She could ride her bicycle to town and continue exploring as she had done on her tricycle, but the real benefit was exploring the farm and roller-skating on the expansive wraparound front porch. In the huge barn's loft, she swung on a long rope, landing on mounds of soft hay.

Patti lived on that farm for one year, and life was mostly pleasant—except for her mother's increasingly erratic behavior, which Patti could generally tolerate. She said, "I was a spoiled child, and Grandmother indulged me with about whatever I wanted."

Sharon Triplett Cotton, a childhood companion who still remains Patti's friend, recalled how Patti's grandmother purchased the young girl expensive Jansen outfits, one in each color. "Her grandmother bought her lots of things. Patti got her way."

More and more, Patti's mother took to her bed—napping, her mother called it. For a time Patti thought nothing about it. Perhaps her mother was merely tired, working too hard. (Seen from today's perspective, her mother was clearly depressed, a condition that now can be treated with therapy and/or drugs.)

Carol Hutchinson Scott, Patti's teenage and current friend, said when she first met Patti's mother, Mary "was taking a nap. It didn't seem right that Patti and Mary were in the same family." According to Scott, "Patti's grandmother was nothing like Mary. Her grandmother was a kind person. Just like Patti."

But one incident completely tripped Patti's switch. She brought home a friend from school whom she wanted to spend the night. Pulling Patti aside, her mother said the girl was not allowed in their house because her family was "unrefined and not suitable to be here." Patti had to tell her to go home. Since her relationship with her mother was already strained, Patti could not tolerate her mother's unkindness.

Patti's stepfather took the girl home.

The next day, eight-year-old Patti packed a small cardboard suitcase, stowed it on the bike's basket, pedaled to her grandmother's house, and vowed never to go back. When Patti's stepfather returned from work, he and her mother went to the grandmother's house and discussed what to do with the independent and headstrong child. Patti stayed in a bedroom but heard the three plotting her future. They decided Patti could stay with her grandmother. And, thus, happy Patti was free at last from her mother's stifling influence.

———

Perhaps leaving her mother's house helped set the freewheeling Patti onto an eventual flourishing career—certainly containing plenty of bumps and discouragements along the way—but one in which she never forgot her Seymour roots or the people of her early and teenage years.

Carol Hutchinson Scott and Sharon Triplett Cotton vividly recall Patti's planning and carrying out several trips for the retired "Seymour Girls," *sans* husbands, to different destinations, such as Bentonville, Arkansas, and Eureka Springs, Arkansas. In 2011, Patti proposed the granddaddy of all trips: a five-day venture to New York City in which she included the 1950s Seymour High School cheerleaders. Through the years, they stayed in close contact, and all ten enthusiastically climbed aboard a jet to New York City's LaGuardia Airport for what Sharon Cotton called "five nonstop days of pure enjoyment."

Patti called their Manhattan hotel "a dump" (about which no one else agreed), and with her patented aplomb, she complained to management, thus procuring for the Seymour Girls a free dinner at an adjoining Irish pub and a few complimentary breakfasts. Apparently, an astute business sense often pays dividends. Many stops in New York City included dinner at Sardi's—no freebie this time—and the distinction of standing outside the *Today Show*'s first-floor window in Rockefeller Center displaying a huge poster for "Seymour Girls, 1950s Cheerleaders, Rooting for Joplin." A brief moment of national fame called attention to the recent devastating Joplin, Missouri, tornado.

Sharon Cotton called Patti the "most caring, compassionate person I've ever known." Her short bicycle trip toting the small suitcase away from her mother's home and into the caring graces of her grandmother surely helped nurture the honorable and unselfish nature contained within Patti Penny. If not completely, then someone or something along the way helped form her generous and charitable spirit, and many people over the years have been thankful for that.

2

Hard Times, Solid Footing

DID PATTI PENNY'S ACUTE BUSINESS sense emerge directly from childhood experiences with her family and childhood friends? Did her mother's seemingly indulgent attitude of spoiling her by buying expensive clothes and allowing her a free tricycle run of the Seymour square give Patti her first taste of how businesses begin and flourish? Shouldn't successful businesses be grounded in confidence and a willingness to take chances—and did Patti unconsciously develop an entrepreneurial spirit in those early carefree days? Or was she born with some inherent and mysterious business DNA, predestining her from the beginning? Seems unlikely. Because many types of personalities venture into business start-ups, and who's to say who is *exactly* the right or wrong person to start a business or what is the best way to begin?

Start-ups face high uncertainty and encounter what some economists call "affordable loss," an almost certain downturn expected with fledgling businesses. Such potholes and bumps along the road might discourage entrepreneurs who haven't planned well and envisioned what could happen, especially at the beginning. Paul Graham, investor in Y Combinator, stated in *TechCrunch,* "What I tell founders is not to sweat the business model too much at first. The most important task at first is to build something people want. If you don't do that, it won't matter how clever your business model is."

Patti Penny's foresight and insight into building a business around people's urgent needs—immediate employment at a decent wage—served her well from the beginning and, thus, thrust Penmac into the success it became and continues to be.

But where in her early Seymour, Missouri, years did her understanding of how to empathize with people's wants and needs originate? Perhaps striking out on her own—keeping a safe distance from her mother—might have fostered her independent spirit, which is vital to opening a business, especially one run by a woman. Enlightening research done by Illuminate Ventures shows that "women [entrepreneurs] have the advantage in some aspects: that women-led companies are more capital-efficient, and venture-backed companies run by a woman have 12 percent higher revenues, than others."

Obviously, the young Patti, while living on the farm with her grandmother, was not aware of such current research into female entrepreneurial start-ups, but a spark inside her later ignited and inspired the adult Patti Halbert Penny to venture into the unknown.

————————

Patti says, "My grandmother was by far the most influential person in my life. This woman, Dorcas Stephens Jennings, had a strong will and possessed an enduring work ethic." The beautiful, black-haired, sixteen-year-old Dorcas Stephens who married Everett Jennings in 1913 lived what appeared to be a charmed and privileged life. Everett Jennings's father, Hiram, was president of the Bank of Seymour and later moved to Springfield to become an officer in the Union National Bank, leaving his son to be president of the Bank of Seymour. Times were good for the couple. Besides running the bank, Patti's grandfather was also an excellent stockman, making much money trading in white-faced cattle and mules. Today, two of his mule barns still stand in the Seymour area,

Patti said, "My grandfather had a generous heart, making many bad loans. In short, he was not a good banker." Then the Great Depression engulfed the country, sweeping thousands of innocent people into debt, pervasive poverty, and hopelessness, including the businesses and outlying farms of Seymour. One need only view class pictures of schoolchildren before and during the Depression to notice how wan, thin, and impoverished the Depression left Seymour children. A drought hit, which devastated crops and Patti's grandfather's cattle business. People were actually starving, causing cattle growers to drive livestock to Diggins, Missouri, to be butchered and turned into canned meat, which was given away to the Seymour Commodity House. The bank closed in 1939.

Patti's grandparents were no longer nestled comfortably in their pre-Depression lives. Like most of the country, they were floating in despair and helplessness. Adding to the sudden bleak times, the anguish of alcoholism swept Patti's grandmother. Her husband fought an enduring battle with drinking. For several years, he tried to stop drinking. He even went to Hot Springs, Arkansas, to "take the waters," which some thought might help, but, of course, it did nothing to address the heart of the issue.

He continued drinking, much to the distress of those around him, especially Grandmother, who said he "went to bed with the bottle." A doctor in Seymour prescribed phenobarbital, which is sometimes given for detoxification. But after the injections in

November 1939, her grandfather did not wake up the next morning. Grandmother was left nearly penniless.

Thus, Grandmother remained with her son, Sam, to manage the farm. Neither knew the ins and outs of farming, but with the help of a hired hand, Ed Anderson, the operation survived. However, like so many farms of that time, it did not flourish.

Finally, after graduating from high school, Sam joined the Army Air Corps, leaving Grandmother and Ed on the farm. Alone. A widow and single man, with the eyes and ears of Seymour watching and listening. For a time, the two thought there was nothing unusual about their situation—until the gossip managed to reach them in dribs and drabs. Did the two know each other conjugally? Or was such a thing merely a result of the town's imagination? Whatever happened, it didn't take long for the gossip to spread. Grandmother said, "The only reason we got married was to shut 'em up." Like her previous husband, Ed was also a heavy drinker who, when drunk, often verbally abused her. Alcoholism, again, became a scourge that Grandmother endured.

Soon after Patti's birth, Grandmother was forced to sell the remaining land she and her first husband owned, keeping a few milk cows. Patti's mother, Mary, left to work at Camp Crowder military base in Neosho, Missouri, because a beauty shop had advertised for hairdressers.

Baby Patti stayed with her long-suffering grandmother. Times were hard. Cows needed to be milked. A baby needed to be looked after. Grandmother moved to the old store building at Sarvis Point because it was the only place she could have her milk cows. When the child was only a few months old, Grandmother walked a quarter mile to the milk barn with Patti on her hip and placed her on an improvised bed while she milked the cows by hand. Many suggested the infant should be placed in an orphanage, but Grandmother refused.

Mary returned, taking the two-year-old Patti and

Grandmother to the beauty shop on the Seymour town square. At the end of the war, Grandmother and Ed Anderson moved to what appeared to be useless land they called "the sprout patch" and managed to eke out a meager living.

Grandmother was always present in Patti's life. Having little money, Grandmother nonetheless saved enough "egg money" to buy Patti beautiful holiday dresses and keep an account at the drug store where Patti could eat whatever she wanted. In many ways, country people were more fortunate than city dwellers in the lean years because of their large vegetable gardens. Grandmother canned most everything from her huge garden. A smokehouse contained cured hams and bacon.

Grandmother wore homemade print dresses. When going to Springfield, she wore one expensive, classy suit, matched with hat and gloves. She was famous for her "mile-high" angel food cakes, which Patti loved. Electricity through co-ops became more and more available to rural areas, and in 1949, for the first time, Dorcas and Ed enjoyed electricity. One of the first things Grandmother bought was an electric mixer, which, by the way, Patti still uses.

Electric mixer or not, Grandmother made a mile-high cake for Patti's birthday and took it to school for the class to enjoy. That treat turned into a tradition for Patti and her classmates. One birthday, Patti eagerly waited for Grandmother to enter dressed in her expensive suit, hat, and gloves. The teacher knew the ritual, as did the class, and as they anticipated the grand entrance, not much serious work got done. Everyone loved Grandmother's easy manner, welcoming smile, and mile-high cakes. This time, Grandmother had told Patti she would bring two. She was always there when she said she would be, but minutes passed while both teacher and students waited, pretending not to notice. Patti waited in her blue velvet dress, the one Grandmother just bought, the birthday dress.

As Grandmother had placed the cakes on the front seat of the pickup and began driving, they started sliding, and when she took her hands off the wheel, she lunged for the cakes. The pickup veered off the road and struck a tree. The cakes lay on the floorboard, smashed, unfit for any birthday celebration, let alone for eating. Grandmother had also slid onto the floorboard.

Almost an hour passed, as Patti, the teacher, and classmates slowly realized there would be no party that day. Finally, the door opened, and Grandmother came in with noticeable scratches and her broken glasses perched precariously on her face. She had bought two coconut cakes, and the class cheered.

Patti, proud in the new dress, walked up to her smiling grandmother—the selfless woman fulfilling her yearly duty—and said, "I knew you'd be here."

"Wouldn't miss it," Grandmother said as she set the cakes on the teacher's desk, "Here, let's all have some cake."

And they did. The tradition still unbroken.

Throughout the years, Ed Anderson's drinking continued. The young Patti endured his rages as well as she could, gazing at a picture on the wall when she felt most frightened: a shepherd tending his flock. Today Patti recalls the strength and courage that picture imbued her with through those times. "Actually, my faith began then, the picture offering me hope."

During one of his drunken rages, Patti and Grandmother left, got a sleeping room in Seymour, and ate canned Vienna sausages off a cardboard box. However, without anywhere else to go, they eventually went back.

Patti said, "He was a hard worker, good farmer, and loved Grandmother. But when he drank, he became a different person." Patti avoided him and kept her distance. Grandmother would eventually leave her husband and move to her own house. She told Patti, "For the first time, I was free from Ed's alcoholism."

In 1938, on a trip to the poor mining town of Martin, Kentucky, Patti's mother visited relatives and met the man who was to become Patti's birth father, Forrest Halbert (whom Patti never met). They married and Mary became pregnant (or vice versa?). Mary told Forrest she was from a well-off family in Seymour, Missouri, but Forrest immediately saw her family was anything but wealthy—and left.

As Patti grew up, she asked about her father, and Mary always spoke in glowing terms, even amorous ones, about Forrest. "He was very handsome and lots of fun to be around." Mary told her daughter many stories about him, including a time in Kentucky when he had two teeth knocked out by a man wielding brass knuckles. Mary especially liked that one. Later, Mary received word Forrest married a nurse, and Patti recalls Mary speaking of her snidely and cruelly.

Mary dated a wealthy attorney in Seymour, Homer Chaffin. Patti said, "My mother liked him because of his money." Chaffin later achieved notoriety in town when Charlie Bruce shot and killed Tom Cantrell during a poker game. Homer defended Charlie Bruce and eventually "got him off" as most Seymour residents put it. The jury was not convinced he had committed murder.

After Homer Chaffin died, Patti said, "My mother then went on the hunt for another man." This time, it was Bill Boring, who was home in Seymour on military leave. Good-looking and five years younger than Mary, they married in El Paso, Texas. Patti said, "He bought me a Mexican top and skirt, which I loved. He told me later that when he saw me for the first time, I was wearing a white rabbit coat, hat, and muff. He said he had never seen a child so beautiful." Patti called him Dad.

When Patti was seven years old, Mary sold her beauty shop,

and they moved to the Kanel farm with Kenny, Patti's half brother. Patti stayed with her mother and Bill for one year, but the quiet and reserved Bill Boring was not much of a farmer. And even if he had been, as he tried making a living with milk cows, the entire herd became infected with a disease—and they all had to be destroyed. It was a huge financial loss. And if that weren't enough, even though he possessed a will from his grandfather giving him ownership to the farm his father and stepmother were living on, the conniving couple used nefarious legal actions to wrest the farm from him because he had no money to fight in his legal defense.

Bill Boring's wealthy uncle, Dean Lewis, owned a car agency in Pasadena, California, and his uncle encouraged them to move to Southern California. Mary was hoping for greener pastures since the Missouri pastures had turned brown and desolate. Alas, Bill bounced from job to job in California and was never able to prosper there.

Mary, according to Patti's description, "thought she had been dropped into heaven." The charming and beautiful Mary Boring landed a job in a beauty salon called "The Head Hunters" in Laguna Beach. She bragged to Patti that "movie stars galore came into the shop," but no specific names were ever mentioned. Mary earned a California beautician's certification, which allowed her to shampoo but not cut or style hair as she had done in Seymour. Still, she was content.

As the years passed, Bill never successfully held down many jobs, and the couple moved back and forth from California to Missouri for Bill's various manufacturing jobs. Patti's brothers, Kenny and Paul, accompanied Mary and Bill on their various moves. Kenny graduated from Orange Coast College and then was drafted while the Vietnam War raged. Paul, according to Patti, "became a full-blown hippie."

After thirty-five years of marriage, Bill Boring discovered

Mary was having an affair with a cousin in Kentucky. And that was it: an immediate divorce.

Patti said, "Dad was free at last." However, he could barely support himself with the small military pension he received after being medically discharged years before. He managed to buy a house in Forsyth, Missouri, and became a regular denizen in several bars, fraternizing with many females he encountered there and living a life of his own making.

Years later, while he was in declining health, Patti, now operating Penmac, took him to the VA Hospital in Fayetteville, Arkansas, for hernia surgery, but he never fully recovered. He did not stop smoking or drinking, and his blood pressure soared. He died two days before his eighty-first birthday.

Patti said, "I thought the world of Dad, and I certainly understand why he couldn't live with Mother."

Deaths, divorces, hard times, and alcoholism riddled the lives and clouded the experiences of Patti's forebears—those she knew and did not know. She recalls much of the past she was told and the past she encountered with a nearly encyclopedic memory. Thus, as she relates detail after detail, one wonders if she has laid out a vivid mosaic of her past that somehow positively informs her present. Has she taken the raw material and shaped it into what her life has become? Possibly so. Yet, she also, like so many of the people from her past, has lived through insecurities and defeats. Any successful businessperson has.

3

Let's Dance

THE UNITED STATES IN THE 1950s was largely united, at least compared to the forthcoming 1960s and 1970s. Many historians described the time as the "simple fifties," and many Americans enjoyed a mostly quiet and settled existence. The mood of Seymour, Missouri, in the poor southern part of the state, was largely no different. The Korean War had just ended after three years and one month, and a new wave of soldiers returned.

In 1953, when Patti Halbert began the eighth grade, the national yearly inflation was 0.82 percent, a gallon of gas was twenty cents, and the cost of a new car averaged $1,650. The novel idea emerged of "buy now, pay later," which allowed many Americans to purchase cars and appliances with long pay periods. That optimistic notion would stimulate the economy and improve people's lives, but it also would lead to long-standing debts for consumers and the nation at large. However, the 1950s were not the times to worry over such matters. Times were good—and safe.

President Eisenhower inaugurated the bold notion of a

national highway system, which later in 1956, would burgeon into the far-reaching interstate highways. Seymour remained relatively isolated, and changes happened slowly. But the optimistic 1950s had a profound effect on the area, especially with the young ones, those of junior high and high school age. Patti Halbert and her friends—"leaders of the twenty-first century" as the popular TV show *Mickey Mouse Club* would label them—entered the new era boldly and hopefully.

Still, not all was bright. In 1953, the USSR tested its version of the H-bomb. A worldwide weapons buildup began that would morph into the long-running Cold War, pitting the economic system of capitalism against socialism and the political systems of communism against democracy. Tensions escalated. Those paying attention worried, but others bounced along with the seemingly carefree 1950s, ignoring such things as the communist-hunting Joseph McCarthy Senate hearings or the rise of Nikita Khrushchev following Joseph Stalin's death.

"Under God" was added to the Pledge of Allegiance, Hugh Hefner's *Playboy* magazine first hit the newsstands with Marilyn Monroe as the nude centerfold, the Salk polio vaccine received full approval, and *Brown v. Board of Education* ruled against school segregation.

For Patti, her grandmother, and Ed, the 1950s were not the best of times. The Midwest suffered a devastating drought in 1953–1954 with the heat sucking water from the ponds, farm pastures turning brown, and cattle dying. People walking across what was once verdant grass heard crunching beneath their shoe soles, and dry rubble was everywhere. And if that were not enough, swarms of grasshoppers plagued what crops remained, turning field corn into ribbons of riddled stalks. The ravenous grasshoppers even munched on the tops of wooden fence posts. "Ed and Grandmother," said Patti, "came through the bad times better than others because they did not have debt." Still, it was hardly an auspicious beginning for what would later become better times.

After Grandmother and Ed acquired electricity in 1949, Uncle Sam returned and bought them their first television in 1951. Patti was eleven years old. They were one of the first in the area to have TV. Patti recalls the proprietor of a radio shop on the square in Seymour putting a television screen in the shop's front window. People would park cars before the shop to watch the black and white snowy screen. Television reception in those early days was fuzzy, at best, with the signal coming from large antennas lodged atop roofs. Patti's television sat in a cabinet with a twelve-inch round screen. They watched *I Love Lucy, Hit Parade, Ozzie and Harriet,* and *Jackie Gleason,* among others. There were only three channels.

They subscribed to a Springfield newspaper. Grandmother would read the paper on the couch after lunch, usually falling asleep doing so. The three never talked about world news, although Patti recalls Ed saying, "If Truman hadn't fired MacArthur, we wouldn't have to worry about Russia now." Her mother was said to have been the only Democrat in the entire county. Most wore "I Like Ike" buttons.

The advent of television had not yet stopped lots of moviegoing. Patti says James Dean was a teenage movie idol, and she and others formed a James Dean fan club in Seymour. Occasionally they made James Dean chili. Why chili? No one seemed to know. His movies, *Rebel Without a Cause, East of Eden,* and *Giant,* enthusiastically drew Seymour teens. However, his career was short-lived, and on September 30, 1955, while traveling to a sports car racing competition in California, his car crashed, killing him. James Dean was twenty-four years old.

The most tragic of all was the plane crash in Clear Lake, Iowa, that killed rock and roll stars Buddy Holly, the Big Bopper, and Richie Valens. Much later, Don Mclean made popular the event in his song "American Pie." Patti said, "In those days we enjoyed being together, usually with a six-pack. None of the girls smoked and drank, but the boys did."

And then there was polio, a dreaded disease that ravished many until the Salk vaccine, and almost every child was immunized. Until then, kids in the summer were discouraged from swimming because polio was mistakenly thought to be associated with summer activities. Al Penny contracted polio in 1955.

In 1954, Patti's freshman year of high school, she engineered what would be the beginnings of her future entrepreneurial spirit. And it started with the Seymour School Carnival, an annual fundraising event where each class tried to outdo the other in raising money. The king and queen of the carnival came from the winning class. The seniors always won, but the 1954 seniors had not seen the likes of Patti Halbert. As a mere freshman, she determined her class would win, an absurd notion. According to Patti, "That presented a challenge to me, so I gathered the troops." She began a massive fundraiser. "I was always the instigator," she said, reflecting on the event and alluding to her later adult efforts. She and her classmates canvassed the area, sold magazine subscriptions and popcorn by the bag for five cents, and collected eggs and burlap bags from farmers to be sold to Seymour townspeople. The freshman class won. "It was my first experience going out into the community asking for money."

Undaunted, Patti took on other high school fundraisers, such as soliciting for new band uniforms since the current ones dated to the 1920s. Then came successful yearbook fundraising. Today she says, "The desire to excel with raising money for special projects stayed with me for the rest of my life."

Fundraising had its rough moments. In an effort to collect money for the March of Dimes—a Franklin Roosevelt project that helped fund polio research—she and others stood on the town square and collected from motorists. An irate citizen wrote a letter to the Seymour paper, complaining about teenage fundraising. "Enough is enough," the writer said. Patti wrote a follow-up letter stating that the March of Dimes was not for Seymour school-related matters; it was for a much greater cause: fighting polio. Nothing more was said.

The Seymour High School mighty freshman class was not finished. The group decided—Patti, of course, was the instigator—that their far-into-the-future senior trip would outshine all the others. Nothing as common as the normal trips to Doling Park in Springfield or Rockaway Beach on Lake Tanycomo—theirs would be the best. Why not shoot for a trip to Miami Beach, Florida? Would they reach the goal? They needed around five thousand dollars. More on that later.

Meanwhile, in the summer of 1954 Patti's father, Bill Boring, heard of a short-term job in St. Louis and one for Patti working at Steak 'n Shake. The family moved—Mother, Patti, Kenny, and Paul—to an apartment on The Hill, the still-famous Italian section of St. Louis. How did the Ozark-born-and-raised Patti react to going from her small town to an urban ethnic enclave? Patti said, "The Hill was filled with great Italian, devout Catholic teenagers. It was a fantastic experience. I had the time of my life. Wonderful, happy people. And I earned enough money to buy school clothes."

How about the shift from hearing and speaking in the Appalachian-based Ozark mode to being immersed in the distinctive St. Louis linguistic patterns, its own dialect region? While Patti certainly noticed the differences, she was charmed with The Hill's vibrancy. Many teenagers' grandparents spoke no English and had no notion of learning.

Patti entered her new friends' quaint bungalow houses and marveled at how they spoke to grandparents in Italian and to her in English. They walked the narrow streets—Magnolia, Reber Place, Daggett, Macklin—and past Yogi Berra's childhood home. At the time, he was playing for the New York Yankees. They heard the Cardinals' radio broadcasts streaming from the houses and small markets. She and her friends visited what is now DeGregorio's market, and Patti stared at the many exotic deli items: mortadella, prosciutto, capicola, and varieties of pasta she had never seen. Her teenage friends drank wine with their families at dinner, a custom so strange as to be unbelievable. Never in Seymour!

She made friends with many teenagers, and Vin Signorelli became her best friend. One boy, Victor Junta, had a convertible with several piling in and cruising Kingshighway into and out of The Hill.

Life on The Hill centered around St. Ambrose Church with the statue of "The Italian Immigrants" in front. Much to Patti's surprise, the parish held teenage dances in the church's basement. She said, "In Seymour, a church would have been the last place to dance." Bill Haley and the Comets had just hit the scene, and the sounds of "Rock Around the Clock" filled the St. Ambrose basement. And, of course, there was fish on Fridays. For the first time, Patti ate pizza, anchovy no less.

She began meeting with the parish priest and taking Catechism classes. "If I had stayed, I would have become Catholic." Her friends who attended Southwest High School, which was close to The Hill, begged her to stay, and she took the idea seriously. However, when she started walking up the long front steps of Southwest High School with the tall Greek statues above the wide portal, she could go no farther. The building was more intimidating than impressive, and she could not bring herself to go in. At the end of the summer, she went back to Seymour to live with Grandmother and her alcoholic step-grandfather.

Thus ended a summer that opened new horizons for Patti Halbert. Later, some of her Italian friends visited her in Seymour, but the tiny town—with no Catholic church—proved unappealing. Yet, her St. Louis memories lasted. She still speaks fondly of those times.

She returned with new ideas that just might bear fruit in Seymour. The American Legion Hall began hosting square dances, and her grandparents managed the concession stand—when Ed was sober. The popular dances attracted many adults but held no interest for teenagers. Then the enterprising Patti Halbert approached the Legion leaders, wondering if they might allow teenage dances. And with enough charm and positive persuasion, Patti won over the Legionnaires, and teenagers filled the hall every Saturday, bringing with them phonographs and 45 rpm records by all the new singers: Elvis Presley, Little Richard, Fats Domino, and The Platters. The Legion provided chaperons who kept sharp eyes out for kids bringing in alcohol, but Patti said, "Someone always brought in beer."

One of the male chaperons eventually went to Patti's grandmother and said the young girl was dancing "too suggestively." Years later, when asked about it, Patti said, "Maybe I was." No more details followed.

Each year, Seymour held horse shows in the local arena, and the popular event drew large crowds, even for Seymour. Patti rode occasionally, but in high school, she joined other young women, dressed in formals—perhaps imitating Southern debutantes—who presented each event's winner a trophy. They were in sharp contrast to the riders outfitted in western accouterments or English riding togs. The arena grounds were laced with excrement from sweaty horses. She stood with her best friends, Helen Stogsdill, Nancy Cornelison, and Liz Davis, all dressed more for a cotillion than a horse event.

Seymour had a movie theater on the square and a drive-in. On hot summer nights, cars loaded with teenagers parked under the stars. Most were paying attention to more engaging activities than watching the large outdoor screen. On a sweltering July night, Patti and Helen sat on the hood of Patti's cousin Delbert's car. Someone, probably Patti, brought up the idea of driving to the tiny burg of Pee Wee, seven miles away, to buy fireworks and visit Patti's friend Nancy, recently married, for a late-night surprise. (Such an event was called a shivaree: a mock serenade with kettles, pans, horns, and other noisemakers given for a newly married couple, mostly southern in origin, the word coming from the Mississippi Valley French, *charivari*.)

Patti and Helen sat on the car's hood, and with typical teenage hijinks, they stayed there—out of the drive-in and onto the road. It was lots of fun, and eleven people were crowded inside and on top of the hood. What could go wrong? Someone had parked a car outside the theater with the lights off to catch a free movie. Delbert plowed into the car, throwing Patti and Helen violently off the hood. Helen sustained a head injury, and Patti, according to her later account, "nearly lost my right leg." All survived. Patti, ever the intrepid one, after much effort, finally learned to dance wearing a cast. Somehow, the music never ended—and the dancing never stopped.

Patti's high school years focused on extracurricular activities, such as cheerleading and band trips. She began as a twirler and advanced quickly to drum majorette because she was tall, and she was class president all four years. Academically, history was her favorite.

What became of that grandiose senior trip to Miami Beach, Florida, that she and her freshmen classmates had aspired to? They raised the five thousand dollars after extensive efforts, and on the night of their graduation, they boarded a Greyhound bus driven by T. D. Wiggs and headed south. Certain classmates were so drunk they vomited in the bus—all boys, Patti says—but their one-week trip was successful. In Atlanta, they visited Civil War sites, and in Pensacola, Florida, they saw the ocean for the first time. Miami Beach was beyond beautiful.

Any dancing there? Perhaps. But it was possibly more of the one-on-one variety. Nothing was officially recorded, and apparently no one was talking.

———

Some things never change as one grows older, and for Patti Penny, her skills and enthusiasm for fundraising continued, especially for Springfield's schools. Her teenage skills in Seymour proved to be only in their infancy stages. As an adult, school fundraising blossomed again. Her older child, Paula, began school at Cherokee Elementary, a country school at the time. Patti joined the PTA, recognizing the school's need for money as the city grew around the school and enrollment increased.

"We became activists for expanding Cherokee because it was becoming too crowded. Of course, we organized. Eventually a bond issue passed, and I made lasting friendships with school district employees. Educational opportunities were very important to me. I realized early on that my education was lacking. I wanted Paula and John to have better."

When Paula and John started at Kickapoo High School, Patti became a PTA leader and sports booster club president. The two duties required much of her time. One of her proudest moments was organizing a spaghetti dinner that raised four thousand dollars. Through her efforts, she and a few others signed a bank loan to buy Kickapoo's first computers.

On the sports front, she and others—spearheaded by Patti— in 1982–1983 organized an alumni basketball game at Kickapoo High School, complete with former cheerleaders like Patti, calling themselves the "High Hookers" and creating cheers, complete with jumps and cheerleader stunts. She said, "Some were more agile than others. I pulled a muscle." Nonetheless, the efforts produced enough funds for a new sound system for the football field and a complete makeover of the baseball field.

From her dancing days in Seymour, as she waltzed through a passion for fundraising, to her adult years of committed and earnest regard for enhancing others' lives—especially a zeal to promote education—Patti's volunteer work helped countless lives. She worked diligently for others as a teenager and continued fervently as an adult—pulled muscles notwithstanding.

4

They Called Her Topaz

IN 1958, EVERYWHERE ACROSS AMERICA, graduating high school seniors were making plans for something, regardless of how foggy their intentions. Some stayed where they were reared and started a life of let's-see-what-happens, proceeding either cautiously, haphazardly, or numbly staring into the first abyss of their lives. Some had definite ambitions and what appeared to be reachable goals, yet exactly how and where to begin eluded them. Some were so idealistic they burst forth optimistically, self-assured, smiling, and ready. Some waited, not actually wringing their hands and tapping nervous feet, but wondering and remaining with parents. Some boarded buses, drove cars, or, if fortunate, climbed into planes and fled the childhood scenes, breathing deep sighs of relief. Some planted roots where they were born, anticipating lives similar to what they had witnessed, hoping a taproot would bury deeply and firmly into familiar soil.

The 1958 Seymour youth fell into any of those categories, not so different from the rest of America's aspiring teens, but always aware that rewarding opportunities might await them somewhere else. Perhaps some feared small-town inferiority that could lead eventually to rigid defensiveness, hidden shame, or benign acceptance of their family's values. And some were so self-assured that they questioned nothing, remembering the secure and mostly prosperous 1950s. For many, a nuclear threat persistently loomed, mushroom clouds perhaps in the distance.

What about Patti Halbert, the leader and instigator of, mostly, positive pursuits and rewarding results? What for her? Stay in Seymour? And do what there? Where to go? To the slightly larger Marshfield in the same county? No, she looked west on Highway 60 to the larger Springfield, Missouri, not only the county seat of Greene County, but the commercial, medical, educational, and entertainment center of southwest Missouri, the place to where she and her mother and grandmother traveled many times during Patti's youth to shop and experience city life. Who knew how many restaurants were there—some she, Mother, and Grandmother had never visited? Most were surely far too expensive for their small-town tastes. And there had been all those special occasions when Patti's grandmother had splurged by buying her clothes in Springfield for Seymour dances or just for walking the high school's hallways. Patti might actually live there and be part of something larger and grander than Seymour.

Should she take such a leap, going from where she had flourished and knew nearly everyone to where she knew no one? And most of all, how would she survive since she insisted on taking no money from her family? Jobs? Maybe she should just hit the streets, hoping perhaps to land a "shop girl's" employment. She had no contacts.

This was Springfield, after all, which dwarfed Seymour and Marshfield put together. In the 1950 census, Springfield's population stood at 66,731 and by 1960, it would increase to 95,865, a 43.7 percent surge, the city's largest leap in the twentieth century. True to form, ever-inquisitive Patti did her research before deciding. She searched the Seymour Library, wanting to know as much as she could.

She learned the territory of Missouri was a part of the Louisiana Purchase of 1804 and that Delaware Native Americans were granted treaty land in what is now Springfield. To the west, Kickapoo Native Americans settled on a prairie that still bears their name. John Polk Campbell, a Tennessean, founded Springfield with the city incorporated in 1838.

Living so close to Springfield, Patti was surprised she didn't know much about the city. She had already read about the tragic Trail of Tears—in the 1830s, the Cherokees were forcibly removed from their homelands in Tennessee, Alabama, North Carolina, and Georgia—but she did not know the trail went right through Springfield and on the way to "Indian Territory" in Oklahoma. She wondered if Springfield had erected a monument to the event.

She learned that the Civil War's Battle of Wilson's Creek was fought just outside Springfield in 1861, one of the first major battles west of the Mississippi River, and another was fought two years later at the Battle of Springfield. After that, the city stayed under Union control until the war's end. On their famous Miami Beach trip, she and her senior classmates had seen several Civil War sites in and around Atlanta. No one had mentioned the Springfield battles.

In Springfield, in 1865, "Wild Bill" Hickok barely ducked a bullet, missing his head, and then shot back and killed Davis Tutt after an argument over a poker debt. She'd never heard her tough-acting male classmates speak of that—and wondered if they knew.

She was shocked to learn of the April 4, 1906, lynching on the Springfield public square of three black men for allegedly sexually assaulting a white woman. The mob broke into the county jail, dragged the men to the square, and hung them from a tower in the center of the square. The black men's employer later testified the men were at work when their supposed assaults took place. No one was prosecuted for the mob's actions. Reading on, Patti learned many black people at the time left Springfield in mass. (The 2010 Springfield census listed whites as comprising 91.69 percent of the population and blacks as 3.27 percent.)

She was only seventeen when she graduated and considered moving to Springfield, but should she really do it? It was a big decision.

Seymour was home, the place where her mother had let her ride a tricycle on the square; the place where she delightfully read books borrowed from the library; the place where she and her young friends watched Saturday afternoon movies at the Owen Theater; the place of many successful fundraisers for the good of her class and the community; and the place of all the horse shows where she and a bevy of high school girls, standing in formals, presented prizes to category winners. Could she leave this town that was full of such significant events and people she had become attached to so firmly?

She had deep roots in Seymour. The first European settlers were Valentine Garner and Jacob Good in 1808, and then in 1818, the town organized and became Seymour. T. Crabbe named it after the Indiana town where he lived before moving west. Patti knew the history. She knew the first newspaper in 1885 was the *Enterprise*—short-lived—changing to the *Sentinel* from 1885 until 1904 and then the *Citizen*, beginning in 1907.

She delved into the archives and learned that in 1907, farm produce, such as rabbits and eggs, was full legal tender at most stores and laughed when she read, "A good preacher or entertainer stood to make as much as $2.50 an evening." In 1936, during the heart of the Great Depression, a person could buy a new Chevrolet at car dealer Smith-Pyatt for $495. Two pounds of crackers sold for seventeen cents, a large loaf of bread for five cents, and five pounds of oatmeal for twenty-three cents.

Her grandmother lived at Sarvis Point, just outside Seymour on the Finley River, and attended many local dance parties in the 1920s and 1930s. Patti had attended the June Singing at Cedar Gap, four miles from Seymour, with the event running continuously for 119 years. In the old days, as many as five thousand people attended. There were also picnics at Finley Falls and fox-hunting at Dogwood.

Much of the history gave Patti added reason to pause and consider an eventual move to Springfield, but she was not one to muse for long over protracted decisions. She would do it. She went—and would stay for the rest of her life. "I never once regretted it."

As things turned out, over the years, she returned her love and affection for Seymour with benevolence and pride. That place would forever remain with her, much to the benefit of grateful citizens.

———

Engaging her stubborn self-reliance, Patti went to Springfield on her own, without a car, determined not to take money from Grandmother and Ed. However, she accepted from her mother and father the first month's rent in a sleeping room at Central and Grant. Her landlady supplied a hot plate, and on that single burner, she fixed whatever food she could concoct, which included lots of Campbell's soup, not exactly Grandmother's fine meals she was used to eating.

Her landlady allowed her to use her refrigerator, a necessity indeed, but it was such a public accommodation—knocking on the woman's door, politely stepping into the kitchen, and retrieving what meager perishables she had bought—that Patti often wondered why she had left the security and privacy of her grandmother's place. She shared a bath with two other renters. Did she miss her more commodious living arrangements back in Seymour? Certainly. Did she ever regret the move? Occasionally. Was she lonely at first, missing her many friends and community acquaintances in Seymour? Indeed. But did that loneliness last long? Thanks to Draughon's Business College, not long.

She walked to Draughon's on Pershing Street, and she met Carol Hutchinson. According to Patti, Carol was there "to escape Mountain Grove, Missouri," which was just a few miles down the road from Seymour. Carol was sixteen and was only there for the summer before she would go back, reluctantly, to finish high school. Later, Patti and Carol rented an apartment on Cherry Street.

Patti had no problem finding waitressing jobs: first at Talk of the Town on Jefferson Street by the YMCA, then at Country Kitchen in the Glen Isle Center, and then at Crank's Drug Store's lunch counter at Cherry and Kimbrough. She left the Crank's job because the tips were small, which was surprising, since Patti's vivacious spirit usually brought enough tips to justify a waitress job. Yet, she said, "The tips at the other places helped me get by."

Could seventeen- and sixteen-year-old girls alone in Springfield in 1958 find entertainment for the summer? Patti said, "We could get into all the bars." Without elaborating much further, she said they "went dancing almost every night." Where? Tumble Inn, Red Barn, Esquire, Pine Room, Star Dust, and Coley's. "To name a few," she said.

Without money to buy new clothes, Patti brought plenty from home. She was the same fashion plate in Springfield as in Seymour: straight skirts with Honey Bun Jensen sweaters, one good pair of heels, a pair of flats, and rock 'n roll shoes with white anklets. For dressy occasions, she and Carol wore sheath dresses with heels, hat, gloves, and purses. They drew plenty of attention around town, both at Draughon's and routinely cavorting each evening. They attracted enough notice that they were asked to model at Springfield's premier department store, Heer's, after taking a Nancy Taylor course at Draughon's, which was taught by Ann Calbert. The Garden Room on the second floor held fashion shows to debut each season's new lines.

They couldn't believe their luck. Just walking into Heer's was enough. It had several floors, a mezzanine overlooking the spacious entry, gold pneumatic tubes shooting cash from a department to the cashier's office and back, and an elevator. The gold door opened with a ding, and an operator in uniform said, "What floor please?" Upon arriving, the operator might say, "Women's furnishings. Watch your step." The enticing cosmetics counter displayed creams and perfumes. At Heer's, they could forget their tiny apartment, scant furnishings, and paltry pay. Seymour and Mountain Grove might as well have been on distant galaxies.

Carol had been dating a boy from Cabool, Missouri, and had a picture of him in their room. Patti withheld telling her she thought the guy was not up to Carol's standards, but finally, after thinking it over, she said she thought the guy looked like Dopey in *Snow White and the Seven Dwarfs*. Patti was certain Carol could do better, and she arranged for her to meet Ronnie Scott from Seymour who according to Patti "was good-looking and a good dancer." Things got serious between Carol and Ronnie, and they eloped in July 1960, leaving Patti without a roommate. To this day, Patti and Carol Hutchinson Scott remain close friends.

Sharon Triplett came to Springfield from Seymour to attend radiology school. Sharon's mother said the two could room together only if they lived at the YMCA, where a strict midnight curfew existed and was enforced. That did not suit Patti. After all, most bars were still up and running at curfew. Patti devised a plan whereby she would plant decoy friends around the front desk to distract the night manager when they waltzed in late. Sometimes it worked, sometimes not, but the enterprising Patti Halbert gave it her best. Always thinking, always planning.

Patti persisted at Draughon's Business College until she finally realized she would not be a secretary (with the eventual hope of making some "real" money). She could barely type forty words per minute, and shorthand was as beyond her comprehension as trying to master nuclear physics. She dropped out and found some part-time jobs, including working the front desk at the YWCA where she took her evening meal at the cafeteria.

Her Seymour boyfriend, Jack Hubbell, had gone to Kansas City seeking work—but found nothing suitable—and then back to Seymour before ending up in Springfield where he and Patti began dating again. Jack knew many local softball players, and they enjoyed going to games, but the biggest thrill of all was the Friday night stock car races at the Springfield Fairgrounds. Upon entering the track's pavilion, she could not believe the noise of the cars as they skidded around the half-mile dirt track. She learned that the races in south Missouri were as popular as in the South, where racing was king. And some of the local drivers became celebrities, such as Don Kordalis and Larry Phillips. (Much later, after marrying Al Penny and when he worked at Lily Tulip, Don Kordalis paid Al to watch his manufacturing machine while he slept under it.)

Jack met Billy Joe Carnahan, who was a friend of Johnny Cash, which impressed Patti, her first brush with "someone who knew someone." And then, on the heels of that, Patti landed a part-time job with the Ozark Jubilee, a Springfield-produced and nationally televised program of country music, square dancing, and comedy. She recalls "having a great time there, all the lights, performers, and excitement of a live television stage show. There was plenty of pressure, but the performers did not show it. Mostly, I was in awe." The Jubilee ran from 1955 until 1960.

During the 1950s, Springfield ranked third in the United

States for originating network television programs, behind New York and Hollywood. The radio networks of ABC, NBC, and Mutual also carried country music shows nationally from Springfield. Staged at the Jewell Theater, Ozark Jubilee was the first national country music television show to feature top stars and attract wide viewership. The show featured well-known performers, including Red Foley, Speedy Haworth, Brenda Lee, Porter Wagoner, Slim Wilson, and Eddie Arnold. John Sellars, executive director of the History Museum on the Square, said, "In those days, Nashville and the Grand Ole Opry were getting nervous. Springfield was having a good run." And Patti was in the middle of it all.

Her job title at the Jubilee? "Idiot Girl." That is, cue card holder. "I put all the words of the songs on poster boards and sat under the camera so the performers could read the lyrics. I did the same for Eddie Arnold, the MC." But the moniker "Idiot Girl" did not last. Patti, in a flight of fancy, colored her hair a golden blonde. "They called me Topaz. A name I didn't mind, but I'm happy it did not stick. Neither did the hair color."

While she worked a part-time job at the front desk of the YMCA, an elderly man who ate evening meals at the cafeteria said he could arrange a job interview for Patti at the stock exchange, which was located in the Landers Building. Should she even try for such an important full-time job? She was still young, and while supremely confident, the thought of even applying left her anxious. But why not apply? She nervously donned her best dress and heels and apprehensively walked to the building. The outer office was small and inviting. The receptionist said the job would be to post all the stock returns on the large chalkboard as they came in. She told the receptionist, "I'm sure I can do that." She waited to be called into the exchange room.

When she entered the overwhelmingly large room, dozens of men were smoking and watching the board intently. She was glued to the floor. The hand holding her purse trembled slightly. A teenager working here? In a place of such importance? All those men looking at her walking back and forth before the board? She turned and went back through the outer office, not speaking to the receptionist, to the safety of a world filled with part-time employment, bars, dancing, and scant money. Wasn't she doing all right as she was? The safety of the street calmed her. Today, she says ruefully, "What a lost opportunity. Think of what I would have learned about stocks!" It was one of her few regrets.

Jobs continued (albeit part-time), and she never stopped looking for additional challenges and, most of all, money to support her new life in Springfield. She landed a menial position in the building that housed the real estate company of R. M. Mack, which was located at the corner of Cherry and National. She did not have a car and took a bus, as she says, "When I could find a quarter." She worked upstairs for Don Simmons who sold life insurance. Unable to afford going out for lunch, she always brought a sandwich, which she ate at Simmons's desk while he lunched elsewhere.

"One day, as I had my tuna fish sandwich spread on his desk, I heard steps coming up the stairs. I jumped up, sandwich in hand, and my foot landed in the wastebasket at the side of his desk. I greeted Don and his guest flat on my face, still holding the sandwich. For years after that, Don never let me forget that moment."

In January 1959, after dropping out of Draughon's Business College the previous month, Patti decided to attend Southwest Missouri State College. Typing and shorthand surely would not be an issue there as they were at Draughon's. She thought things over carefully. She was bright, loved learning, liked to study, and by all indications was the perfect candidate to become the first of her family to earn a college degree. Few people in Seymour had college degrees besides teachers. The thought thrilled her.

She visited the campus. At the time, it had an enrollment of around two thousand, certainly more students attending classes than the entire population of Seymour. Its spacious Carthage stone buildings were nestled in a compact area of town bounded by Monroe, Grand, National, and Kings Streets. The visit brought to mind her time on The Hill in St. Louis where just a few years before she learned to navigate the streets with her friends. She knew she could do this. As she walked up the few steps of Carrington Hall, the administration building, she was not wowed or intimidated as she had been when entering Southwest High School in St. Louis, a building even larger than Carrington. She had turned back in St. Louis, but this time, she was resolute.

Up the stairs she went, found the admissions office, and after hurriedly thumbing through the college catalog and meeting at length with an admissions counselor, she was shown to the Registrar's Office to enroll. With a few part-time jobs in her wake, she had saved enough for the registration fee. By the time classes began, she could, with monthly payments, afford the tuition. She envisioned new beginnings as a college co-ed.

While attending Southwest Missouri State College, Patti worked mornings at R. M. Mack, and then she would go to her rooming house to get her books and go to campus for afternoon classes.

One day, she was late, and a man stopped his car beside her and said, "Need a ride? I'm going to the campus."

Foolishly, she got in the car.

She was barely inside before he said, "I'm taking you out a few miles. You look like you'd like to have some sex."

Her window was down, and the terrified Patti shouted, "Help!"

He said, "Shut up! I'll let you out." He stopped at Grand and Dollison.

Patti immediately jumped out of the car, got his license number, ran to a gas station on the corner, and called the police, giving the phone number of the rooming house where she lived. She waited for a week or two, expecting a call from the police. After all, she had given them the license number. Weeks passed with no word.

Three months later, when she thought the police had completely ignored the incident, a policeman came to her work. "The only charge we can level against the man is disturbing the peace since he didn't touch you."

"Should I press charges?" she asked.

"You have that right."

She thought it over.

"But he is married," the officer said, "and pressing charges would cause him lots of trouble at home."

Her face reddened. "In other words, Officer, you think I should feel sorry for him?"

"Well ..."

"You realize, don't you, that if I had not been able to get away, he might have raped and possibly killed me? I'm not sorry for that man and never will be!"

The office said nothing.

"You want me to protect him?" she asked.

"You may press charges or not."

Patti told him to leave, which settled the issue, but the incident, after all these years, still weighs heavily on her mind. Today, she says, "I suppose it taught me a lesson I should have learned before. Don't be so trusting of strangers. I was young, and I realized I was not living in Seymour anymore."

Patti thought she had saved enough money to buy a car. When she approached her stepfather in Seymour, he went to Medley Motors and found her a 1953 Chevy Power Glide. Since she was a hundred dollars short for the down payment, Ed Anderson kindly supplied it. She was making forty dollars a week now, and her car payment was twenty-nine dollars per month. The car was a boon to her getting around town, and she helped transport several of her car-less friends.

At the rooming house, Patti met a woman who was fifteen years older. Grace Willard arranged an interview for Patti at Lily Tulip in Springfield. The firm at the time had more than 1,600 employees and boosted the area's economy by manufacturing paper cups and lids. It was the largest business of its kind in the country. Located on Glenstone Avenue, the plant sported a giant Lily Tulip cup, an iconic Springfield landmark. Her first job was in the traffic department as a file clerk with the cabinets in the large "cup." It was a difficult surface to walk on, so she removed her heels and filed in stocking feet. She was then moved to a section where she weighed truck and rail cars with containers that were ready to be shipped.

In May 1959, she reluctantly dropped out of Southwest Missouri State College because of her work schedule. "By the time the sun hit the west windows of Lily Tulip, I could barely hold my eyes open. However, at 5:00 p.m. I was ready to go dancing again."

Turns out, she was ready much later to dance herself smack into a major turning point of her life. And being Patti, she was ready for whatever might come her way—or, more accurately, whatever she could make happen.

5

Finding a Penny

FOR MANY PEOPLE, THE 1960S was a pivotal decade of change—not only in the United States but in the world. Some said the ten-year period seemed to march on and on, a never-ending sweep of time bringing change, upheaval, and revolution.

The Cold War of the 1950s heated up well into the 1960s, pitting the United States against the Soviet Union. The long-standing Arab-Israeli conflict morphed into the 1966 Six-Day War between Israel and Jordon, Egypt, and Syria. In 1961, the United States sent seven hundred advisers into Vietnam, followed eventually with five hundred thousand troops, bolstered by the draft. The Cultural Revolution headed by Mao Zedong swept China. In 1962, the United States and the Soviet Union during the thirteen-day Cuban Missile Crisis avoided a near military confrontation just off the coast of Florida. Wars occurred worldwide, including the Indo-Pakistani War and Nigerian Civil War. In the decade, there were eighteen global assassination attempts or killings.

The years from 1963 until 1974—framed by John Kennedy's

assassination and Richard Nixon's resignation—are often called the "Cultural Decade." Significant changes took place in America, mostly brought about by the anti-war movement, the civil rights movement, and what is often termed the sexual revolution. The many changes were manifested in music (Bob Dylan, Joan Baez, Pete Seeger, and Jefferson Airplane), films (*Psycho, 2001: A Space Odyssey, Easy Rider,* and *Rosemary's Baby*), and writing (*A Clockwork Orange, The Electric Kool-Aid Acid Test, One Flew Over the Cuckoo's Nest,* and *To Kill a Mockingbird*).

Still, much of the 1950s spilled into the 1960s, and change did not happen abruptly. Such actors as Doris Day, Audrey Hepburn, Jack Lemmon, and Rock Hudson quietly and graciously slipped into the new decade; the Beach Boys, Supremes, Johnny Cash, and Elvis Presley maintained a cozy alliance with the calmer 1950s; and television still entertained lightly with *Bonanza, My Three Sons, The Wonderful World of Disney,* and *The Andy Griffith Show.*

For many of Patti Halbert's age, the early 1960s did not usher in much new, especially those making personal transitions or trying to step from one life cycle into another. Some were too busy taking care of business, concerned with beginning new roles, from the teenage years into early adulthood; some were just beginning what they hoped would be promising careers; some faced the daily struggles of making ends meet, trying to stand pat; some were without many long-term goals; and some held bold assurances that their carefully planned goals would yield bright futures. Others refused to participate, spurned the upheavals, fought against what they thought was destructive behavior, and tried to right the wrongs they saw proliferating around them.

A few adults today say, "The sixties passed me by. I was too busy to notice." However, a certain famous and facetious remark remains, referring to the prevalent drug use of the time: "If you remember the sixties, then you weren't there."

Regardless of how one experienced the decade, few escaped its broad impact.

———————

With a job at Lily Tulip and, at long last, her car, Patti Halbert would pick up Sharon Triplett and cruise the Springfield drive-ins in the evenings, searching for whatever action might turn up. While her car was not exactly what she called one of the "slick" cars that so many boys of that time prized and sought to show off, she and Sharon placed themselves within the circling caravans, going from one hot spot to another. They favored Fisher's Hi Boy, Taylor's, and Leroy's, and if they were lucky enough to find a parking spot—any one would do—ordering burgers and sodas took second fiddle to chatting up the people in the cars next to them. The loquacious Patti struck up lots of talk, male or female, while Sharon on the passenger side lost no opportunity cozying up to whoever was on her right. They were equal opportunity chatterers, regardless of the people in the cars. After all, they were working girls out on the town, enjoying more freedom than they had ever known.

They made friends, never declining the male invitations of, "You girls wanna ride around?" Patti's Chevy stayed parked at the drive-in while the driver and his passengers patrolled all the drive-ins, stopping at some, often merely driving indiscriminately around, seeing what the night might hold for the carload full of newly found friends. Of those times, Patti says, "We had some good conversations." What kind of conversations? "Oh," she says today, her acute memory suddenly failing her, "just conversations."

One day at work, after a night of "hitching rides," a fellow worker said, "Patti, I heard you were riding around last night."

"Yeah, with Sharon."

"Have a good time?"

"Yeah. This guy driving was really nice. I sat in the front with him."

"Oh."

"He might be a good catch."

"I hope nothing happened between you and him."

"Certainly not."

"Patti, he's my brother-in-law. Married to my sister."

Patti blanched. She recalled the time she was late to class, getting in a car with a stranger and everything that happened after that: the police, the drawn-out investigation, how she might have been harmed.

Her coworker said, "I know you weren't aware of who he is. Sometimes news travels fast."

From then on, Patti and Sharon made a pact not to ride with anyone they did not know well, but it didn't stop them from continuing their nightly drive-in ramblings.

A week later, on a Sunday night, after returning from a weekend in Seymour, Patti and Sharon pulled into LeRoy's for a burger and fries.

Someone in the neighboring car squirted ketchup from a squeeze bottle into her car, just missing her face. And there sat a grinning boy. "Get your attention?" he asked.

"Look what you did to my dress!"

"Sorry."

"Why did you do that?" But she was suddenly amused.

The guy on the passenger side asked, "You girls want to ride?"

She and Sharon looked at each other. "No, thank you," Patti said, not wanting to break the vow she and Sharon had made. The guy who asked didn't say anything. Patti thought he just looked disappointed and slightly sad.

A week later, Patti received a call at the YWCA from some guy named Al Penny, saying he would like to meet her. Still a bit reluctant to engage with someone she didn't know, she said, "I'm dating someone else."

Silence. Finally, he said, "Remember that night at LeRoy's when someone squirted ketchup on you?"

"How could I forget?"

"That was my cousin. I was the other guy in the car."

"The one who asked if we wanted to ride around?"

"Yes."

"Actually, it was pretty funny." She let dead air hang, thinking about her boyfriend.

"What?" he asked.

"Uh, I'm dating someone right now."

"Well, I guess that answers my question."

Silence on Patti's end. Had she heard of his name? Too much to consider while standing there with the phone in her hand.

"I don't want to break up anything," he said. "Best of luck."

He sure seemed like a polite, considerate guy. But then, there was the boy she had always been so happy with. Yet, the one who, she noticed, might be becoming more distant.

The next day at work, she asked around to see if anyone had heard of Al Penny. Checking him out wouldn't hurt anything. A few of the girls knew him because he'd worked there previously. One said, "He's a nice guy, but if you go out with him, be sure to wear your flats."

"Why?"

"Because you might need to walk."

"Why?"

"He has a car. But just in case."

Al's voice on the phone had sounded sincere. Nothing appeared to be up his sleeve. But how much can a girl tell from someone's voice? She'd think this over.

Patti had known her boyfriend in Seymour, had grown up with him, and had dated since high school. After Patti moved to Springfield, he found a good job at a well-known and successful business, Richardson Supply, owned by Hank Richardson. Patti liked Hank and his young family and was delighted when her boyfriend landed such an attractive, well-paying job. Hank liked the boy's work and took him under his wing, just the kind of break Patti knew he needed. And if they should marry, his employment would hold them in good stead.

However, their relationship began unraveling (at least in Patti's mind) when she discovered that Hank was a heavy drinker. With all the effects of alcohol in Patti's past, especially with Ed Anderson, her step-grandfather, she hoped Hank's drinking did not affect her boyfriend's job or the viability of the business. But, most of all, since he did not drink in high school, would he follow Hank's example? Surely not. But could he be easily influenced?

He was. The two men began having "company" parties at such popular Springfield establishments as The Grove and Riverside Inn. Patti wondered if she could tolerate such behavior, but she did because he was good to her, and she to him.

He told Patti of a woman who worked at Richardson Supply who, he said, was mistreated by her husband, which affected not only her, but her two small children as well.

"I feel sorry for her," he said, more than once. "Her husband is nothing but a son of a bitch."

Since Patti had learned that Hank was an alcoholic and an inveterate womanizer, surely her boyfriend would not follow suit, would he? And what about that poor woman at his work? Could he be ...?

He enjoyed bringing the charming Patti to many of Hank's nights out, saying, "Come along. I want to show you off. Let others see what a catch you are." Besides, The Grove was one of the foremost venues in Springfield. Patti observed firsthand a taste of "the good life." She enjoyed herself. Besides, she seemed to be a hit.

One night, he introduced Patti to a woman who had shown up alone. Later, he whispered, "That's the woman at work I've told you about."

The woman made a point of never standing around them, but she appeared to be looking their way more often than Patti felt was necessary.

The next day, the insightful and apprehensive Patti confronted him, saying, "How long have I been a cover for you?"

"What?"

"That woman last night. You've been seeing her, haven't you?"

He didn't hesitate. "I have."

Patti needed to know the truth, but she had never imagined how the truth could bring tears and suddenly cause her to experience—for the first time and so bitterly—the agony of rejection. And under such humiliating circumstances. So much good had always come her way. Then this.

Years later, Patti learned the husband of the woman her boyfriend had been seeing found out about her affair. He shot her, put her body in his trunk, and buried her in an isolated spot with a bulldozer. After much investigation and a well-publicized trial, the man was convicted of second-degree murder and sent to the Fordland Correctional Center. While on a work detail, he escaped and disappeared.

Three days after Patti's breakup, Al Penny called again. Had he heard something? They spoke only briefly about nothing much until he asked if she might change her mind.

"It doesn't even need to be a date," he said. "Just to talk."

She couldn't hold back. "It can be a date."

He paused and then said, "Oh?"

"I'm ready for a date now."

She put on her flats and away they went to the Star Dust, a quieter bar than most. They talked for several hours. She was surprised to learn Al was six years older and, most of all, that he was full of serious plans, always looking forward. And here she was without a college degree, working at a good-enough paying job, but beginning to consider where it was taking her. Sitting there at the Star Dust and observing his calm assurance and drive sparked within her a certain enthusiasm that must have lain dormant for a few years.

He slowly spun his life's story, telling it smoothly and unhesitatingly, like pulling silk off a spool. She listened, not wanting to interrupt—actually unwilling to reveal her shallower future intentions.

He worked at Lily Tulip before she arrived but saw no particular opportunities for advancement. She thought of a saying she'd heard in Seymour: "He doesn't let much grass grow under his feet." Was it her grandmother or mother who said that? He heard of a new company opening in Springfield, Dayco, and with an adventurous spirit—she saw it unfolding right before her—he left Lily Tulip and went there. After a few months, he grew to hate the working conditions. She wanted him to elaborate on that but would not stop him. A new plant opened next door to Dayco, Hoerner Box, and feeling the itch to what he hoped would be a better job, he became their first employee.

"I guess you made more money there," Patti said.

"Less money. A big pay cut. I sensed better opportunities if I just stayed with it. Work myself up."

She'd never heard of leaving a job and taking less money.

"I had to move and live with my sister's family to make ends meet. Things are looking better now."

Such maturity and forethought, she thought.

He became quiet, and she sensed he was entering a new conversation, taking a sidetrack.

"I've been divorced for two years," he said.

Patti wanted to look away, but she didn't and was surprised to see he kept his eyes locked on hers.

"Oh," she said. "I see."

Her mind switched into warp speed, weighing the possibilities and liabilities before her. Fortunately, he had lifted his hand to the server, ordering more drinks, giving her time. Should she tell him she had just broken up? And wasn't that almost like a divorce, without all the legal entanglements? This certainly wasn't the time to inquire into the particulars of his split, and she did not necessarily want to talk about her breakup, but here was this man—yes, a man, not a kid—exuding calm confidence.

Perhaps now was the time to tell him about her job, about coming to Springfield from Seymour. And she did, in just enough detail not to sound airy. He listened, appearing honestly interested, making her want to open up more. But she wouldn't dominate this kind man, as if she ever could.

"I've heard of Seymour," Al said. "East of here, right?"

"It is. Small place."

This made him grin. "I've from Clever. Not much of a place really."

She might have made some clever remark about Clever, but she refrained.

"I should explain more about why I took a job for less money. I was raised poor. Had to work for every penny."

"Your name," she said. "Penny."

"It's fitting."

Did she catch him blushing? Then he laughed. "I'd never made that connection."

She sipped her fresh drink while he continued.

"I was raised extremely conservative about money."

Patti wondered if she were reared that way too—or did she grow up having more than he?

"If I wanted a bag of candy, Dad made me pick up rocks from our fields and toss them into a wagon."

Nothing like that in Patti's past. She thought of all the new clothes her grandmother lavished on her, clothes she still wore.

"He paid me a nickel a load."

Was he making this up, trying in some odd way to impress her?

"Is this boring you?" he asked.

"It's fascinating. Honestly, I've never heard of anything like that."

"Want me to stop?'

"No! Go on."

He said when he was fifteen, he wanted a car, thinking by some odd chance, his father might lend him the money, knowing he'd never hand it over free. His father said Al could work for it. He led his son into a field and marked off what they thought would be about an acre. "You can grow something here," his dad said and then walked away.

"About the only things I ever worked for," Patti said, "were charity fundraisers. Nothing like what you say."

"I always worked and still am."

Did he mean this condescendingly? Surely not. "What did you do with that acre?" she asked.

"I decided to grow cucumbers."

"On a whole acre?"

"First, I had to clear the ground to get it ready for planting. Not easy work."

Out of nowhere, Patti wondered about his divorce. Who was the woman? Why did they split? Were they as poor as he was while growing up? Now, he was saying something about how fast cucumbers grew.

"I had to pick them a certain size—or the processing plant wouldn't take them."

"So," she said, "you couldn't let them get too big?"

"Right. I worked every day."

"We had a processing plant in Seymour," she said. "For tomatoes."

"Did you work there?"

"No."

"Did you raise tomatoes?"

"No." She had interrupted his story for no reason. "Did you get the car?"

"Yes. I finally bought one."

He said his father asked how he would maintain the car. Al hadn't thought of that. So his dad said Al could help milk the cows, and they would weigh the milk of one cow each day, thus earning the money from that cow. Problem was, Al played basketball, and if he missed the milking because of practice, his dad would not weigh the milk. On top of that, when the weekly milk check came in, Al had to ask for his portion or his father would not relinquish it.

They stayed at the Star Dust until almost closing, and Patti learned more about Al Penny than she could have imagined. And she had said hardly anything.

In the parking lot, Al asked if they could see each other again. They did. Again and again.

Grandmother Dorcas Jennings, c. 1943

Patti and husband Al standing before Al's 1956 Ford convertible.

Wedding day, December 31, 1960

Mother Mary 1944

Patti, six years old, 1946

Daughter Paula, four months old, October 1962

Majorette, 1957

NYC Central Park

Horse Show 1957 -- Patti far left.

left to right, The Penny Family: Paula, Al, Patti, John
(ca. 1970s/early 1980s)

Closing of the Sale of Penmac: left to right, Al, Patti, John,
attorney Frank Carnahan, Jennifer (John's wife), Paula

6

Adjusting and Settling

THE COUPLE WASTED NO TIME. Their first date at the Star Dust was in September. In November, Al proposed marriage at Fisher's Hi Boy while sitting in his car, just after ordering their usual burger and fries. Patti sensed this might happen because on a couple of occasions, she had ushered their conversations rather obliquely toward the word *marriage*, tiptoeing just enough, she thought, for Al to catch the subtlety. Was that why that night at Fisher's he had ordered shakes for both of them—chocolate for her, vanilla for him? Definitely a bold menu move for the frugal Al. She might have guessed a proposal was coming, but at Fisher's?

During their brief dating months, she wondered if they would even be a good match for marriage. She was a spender; Al was a saver. Would his family's austere ways and his own spartan work habits turn him into a miserly husband or, dare she say it, a penny-pincher?

Her breakup with her boyfriend was still raw in her mind—more so than she cared to admit—and she couldn't escape the notion that if they married, and if things turned sour, and if, heaven

forbid, their love waned, a divorce could ensue. There could be
no need for staying in a troubled marriage.

But right there, with cars parked beside them and carhops
bustling around, he asked. Good thing she had just set her shake
down on the window tray; otherwise, she might have dropped the
blessed thing on her skirt, not out of surprise, but sheer happiness,
perhaps even relief.

"Of course I will!"

Never a squealer, she surprised Al and the people in the
adjoining cars—who were probably wondering what had just
happened. All they saw was some startled guy engulfed in a girl's
embrace. Without so much as the classic get-down-on-your-
knees proposal, she held Al for the longest time. Who needed that
traditional nonsense anyway, especially from Al, who probably
couldn't have executed it if he tried? It was all perfectly fitting
there in his beloved 1956 Ford convertible. And with Fisher's Hi
Boy customers as their witnesses.

She didn't want to mention a ring because she knew he had
little money, and she certainly didn't have much. As if to read
her mind, when she released him from her long hug, he said,
"Tomorrow, let's go to Fayman's ."

She knew all about Fayman's Jewelry, but she had never been
there. Although without telling him, she had on the sly browsed
through Hocklander's Jewelry, sizing up wedding bands just in
case he might broach the possible engagement question. That
way, she'd be a step ahead. But knowing their precarious financial situations—if you could even label their meager incomes as
"financial"—her perusal quickly discouraged any realistic notion
of a diamond engagement ring. Still …

"At Fayman's to look for rings?" she said, stating the obvious.

His broad smile told her he might know something she didn't,
but at that point, that was not what counted most.

"Hey," she yelled so that people three cars down could hear. "Guess who's getting married—and guess who just found out?"

Someone honked a car horn, and then others picked it up. Carhops clamored at the sudden blaring noise, and the manager peeked through the service window. Soon, almost everyone knew about the couple in the Ford convertible.

"Show me your ring," a smiling girl in the neighboring car said.

"Come here this time tomorrow," Patti told her and lifted her left hand, pointing to her ring finger. Then she looked at Al who was still smiling, but not so widely. Maybe he didn't have the ready cash just yet. Maybe they would only be looking, shopping for the best deal, in typical Al fashion.

But she wouldn't dare tell Al those thoughts at this place. Instead, as the horns died down, she leaned over to kiss him, and in doing so, one long leg shot up and slammed onto the window tray. Her chocolate shake fell and crashed on the pavement.

Al seemed hardly to notice as his fiancé's kiss lingered longer than usual.

When learning of their engagement, Patti's mother said, "Does this guy have a bank account?"

Patti was not surprised since her mother's measure of suitable male material was having plenty of money on hand, ready to be spent.

Her grandmother, however, said, "I just want you to be happy, Patti." A characteristic response.

Her mother's initial reaction was probably valid. The couple was scarcely able to come up with thirteen dollars apiece for wedding bands at Fayman's. They did have jobs, but they had barely enough money to survive. And what about a place to live? They began concocting plans.

Remembering the times, Patti said, "We wanted to make fast plans to buy a house."

Al seemed to have the most logical idea. They would ask his father for a loan, which made Patti downright nervous. She had met Al's father, but actually standing before him and asking for money? She had no idea how he might react, but the confident Al plunged right in.

"Dad knows I believe in working. He's seen me work for money."

"I hope you're right."

And he was. After learning how much money Al had in savings—a surprise to Patti, even though she knew he was frugal—his father agreed to a loan of two thousand dollars. Patti knew better than to ask how they would pay him back since they both made only forty dollars a week. Yet, she placed faith in her fiancé.

In December, they found a one-bedroom house in Springfield on West Nichols with five acres and a barn. The area was mostly populated with retired families from the Frisco Railroad.

They would be wed at the First Baptist Church in Seymour, so it was Patti's responsibility to make the arrangements. She borrowed a wedding dress and bought a new pair of shoes and a hat. What about flowers? Certainly no money for that.

Sharon Triplett had an idea. "My parents have easy access to all the flowers you need."

"How so?"

"Think about it."

Sharon's parents managed the funeral home in Seymour. There were always flowers at funerals.

A day later, Sharon said, "My parents would be glad to provide the flowers—a wedding gift."

Patti nearly cried, and then she looked at Sharon. "Funerals and weddings. What a connection!"

Sharon was the maid of honor, and Al's cousin, Jerry Geren, (the ketchup-squirting guy) was best man. Since Patti did not want her mother to attend—disagreements and hard feelings had littered their relationship for years—she did not invite any of her family, not even her grandmother, a decision she regrets to this day.

As the bride and groom strode up the aisle, legally and happily married, Patti saw her young brother Kenny outside, his face pressed against the front door's window. He had been shut out from his sister's wedding.

For the wedding reception, the couple's friends planned a New Year's Eve party in Springfield at Half a Hill dance club. They welcomed in the New Year and new marriage doing what they always loved: dancing with their friends.

Why did they marry on New Year's Eve? Al said they could claim a marriage deduction on their taxes for the whole year, which was a real bonus. Patti hadn't thought of that, but since Al Penny was always Al Penny, he certainly had. Maybe it was a lot like the benefits of raising cucumbers on an acre of ground. Other benefits? They were in love—and they stayed that way.

Thus began a new decade for the newly married couple, one in which they could never imagine what changes were to come. After all, it was the 1960s.

Patti continued working at Lily Tulip, and Al continued at Hoerner, advancing slowly. How did "Patti the spender" get along with "Al the saver" in those early years? As well as could be expected. According to Patti, "We basically didn't spend anything." At least by her standards. After all, she still wore the fine clothes her grandmother had bought for her, and even though, out of Al's gaze, she window-shopped aplenty, she managed not to indulge. How could she?

They barely eked by, and Al kept up his provident ways with money. Patti called it closefisted and stingy, but each week, they deposited cash into an account that was off limits for withdrawal. To Patti, it seemed like the key could never be found.

They occasionally had words about their philosophy of monetary differences. Patti attempted to stand her ground for as long as she could, and the usually reticent Al firmly insisted the account "was for their own good" and that "someday you'll see its value." Just when would *that* day come?

Yet, they were a "happy enough" couple. Patti was glad Al joined the Hoerner bowling league at Holiday Lanes, getting together with fellow employees once a week. Bowling didn't cost much. He worked hard and deserved some freedom, and she enjoyed her time alone each week.

One time, he invited her to go with him.

"You know, I'm not much of a bowler, and besides, I'm not on the team," she said.

"But you can meet some of my friends."

She remembered the bowling alley was next door to a Ben Franklin store. Al introduced Patti to his friends, and after watching for a short while, knowing that league bowling took some time, she drifted out unnoticed to the store next door. Walking up and down aisles merely looking beat watching bowling any day.

In the cleaning supply aisle, she picked up some kitchen cleanser and two sponges. They needed the items, and God knows they could at least afford that much. The bathroom was starting to look a mess, so she couldn't resist the tile-scrubbing brush. One more kitchen hand towel with the embroidered pattern would liven things up. They'd talked about having friends over for Rook, so why not a brightly patterned throw for the couch?

The seven dollars in her purse barely covered it. Al would be pleased she had bought so wisely and economically. She placed her purchases in the car and showed them to Al on the way home.

"Just a few things from the Ben Franklin," she said. "Gussy things up a bit."

One by one, she pulled them from the bag, narrating along the way, telling him just where each would go.

"Say something." she finally said. It was like he wasn't even in the car.

"This week's grocery money?" he asked, looking at the road ahead.

To make their finances work, they had decided on a strict weekly budget. Patti was in charge of buying the groceries. Seven dollars a week. This was Monday.

"Oh my God, Al!" Why hadn't she thought of that?

She watched his jaw muscle tighten.

"I'm so sorry." She had broken a practice they'd both agreed upon. It ranked much higher than a formality, but it had become a way of life in the early days of their marriage. Something she had assented to. It was almost like lying.

"Patti, this will turn out to be a small thing."

Apparently, he was thinking of their future together, imagining their lives on down the line, all the events and circumstances yet to come.

Years later, she said, "It is hard to describe what a wonderful husband Al has been. He is my rock."

But the Ben Franklin episode still carries a certain amount of regret—even if it shouldn't.

The nearly locked-and-sealed savings account, at least on the withdrawal side, continued growing with monthly, often weekly, deposits. They were determined to pay back Al's father for the two thousand-dollar loan, and they did so within a year. It was an amazing feat, considering their austere existence, and it would lead to a mind-set for the rest of their marriage: attempting to keep debt at a minimum. (Now in their fifty-ninth year of marriage, they have bought only one new car, both seeing new cars a waste of money.)

Suddenly, Al's father proposed a deal for the young couple. As a cattle farmer, he offered them his baby calves to wean and, thus, would let them have the bull calves to sell. This would be Patti's first foray into any kind of farming venture, let alone a business enterprise. Should she trust Al on this? What if the plan should prove entirely too much work without sufficient return?

Al said, "We would need some kind of truck to manage such a thing. Hauling calves here and there."

It was all new stuff for Patti. Their newly acquired determination not to enter unnecessary debt at first blocked them. Buying a pickup would require a loan. Was it worth the debt?

The next morning, before leaving for work, Al said, "I can sell my car—then buy a pickup."

This was Al's beautiful 1956 Ford Convertible, the very car in which he proposed, the car that was so admired while cruising Springfield, people commenting on it, especially at the drive-ins.

"Oh, Al, you can't."

And they both must have arrived at the same conclusion, but it was Al who put it into words. "How many times have we gone to Fisher's lately?"

He had a point.

"We can make some money with the cattle," he said.

"But your car?"

Perhaps the reality of what a married couple must do to make the necessary new and strange adjustments struck them full force. They sold the car, bought the pickup, and went into business together. Maybe a person had to start somewhere. The calves helped supplement their meager income. It was plenty of work, but were the new venture and the time spent worth the effort? Perhaps not, but they stayed with it. There were not many other options. Was it the beginning of a nascent business model?

The tiny house on Nichols Street was sparsely appointed with secondhand furniture, hand-me-downs from Patti's grandmother, and the odd piece picked up here and there. The haphazard decor suited them well since Patti and Al had made a pact to become financially stable. The spare furnishings were part of their larger scheme for independence by avoiding unnecessary debt.

Food was certainly nothing elaborate—or what some might call high cuisine—but Patti, as the young bride, wanted to establish some kind of culinary standard. Maybe she would try something besides the usual hamburgers and chili; something as traditional and homespun as fried chicken should be simple enough.

Buying a whole chicken was no problem (few stores in those days stocked cut-up chickens, and asking a butcher to do it might be more expensive). She would serve mashed potatoes with the standard accompaniment of green beans and a simple lettuce salad. Should she economize by making her own salad dressing instead of purchasing bottled? Grandmother always made her own, as far as she could remember, but exactly how she did it and with what ingredients completely escaped Patti. Rolling down the condiment aisle, she wanted a dressing Al would like. French would do. Oh, and the cooking oil for the frying pan, which was an old, well-seasoned cast-iron one her grandmother gave her. Strange how much she did not have on hand for a proper chicken dinner. She'd need flour for coating each piece before frying, two cans of green beans, five pounds of potatoes, and lettuce. The passing thought of dessert whizzed through her head, but she quickly dismissed it.

She stood over the chicken with butcher knife in hand. Now what? She'd never cut one up—having watched Grandmother do it—but how hard could it be? Two legs, two wings, two breasts, two thighs. They were in there, but they were all stuck together.

The result of her work more resembled an odd, mutilated fowl of unknown species rather than your average chicken. Maybe Al wouldn't notice. Then again, maybe he knew how to do it and possibly already mastered it in his past, the farm boy he was. Peeling and cutting up the potatoes went smoothly, and as they boiled, she set the chicken to frying, the green beans on low to simmer. Then completely unbidden, the word *gravy* visited her, a part of the whole procedure so far beyond her competence as to be nearly humorous. But things were coming together when Al walked in.

"Do I smell chicken frying?" he asked, pecking her on the cheek as she tried to shield him from peering into the skillet.

"Thought I'd surprise you," she said.

But as he looked into the frying pan, he said, in his usual droll way, "Yep, a surprise all right."

Patti knew what he meant, but instead of taking offense, she gently pushed him away, trying not to smile. "Mashed potatoes and green beans with the chicken," she said.

From the other room, he said, "How will you mash the potatoes?"

She had no potato masher, something she'd never considered, and quickly pondered some improvisational tool that might work. She finally admitted mashed potato defeat. "Did I say mashed?" she asked. "I meant boiled."

While Al complimented her on the meal and ate what turned to be, he said, well-prepared chicken, Patti could only stare at what she'd fixed, thinking mostly of the hacked-up bird.

While they could not afford to go out to eat often, they located a small place on College Street, Piggs, which served a complete meal for eighty cents.

"Wanna go to Piggs tonight?" one of them might ask.

"Sure."

They filled the nonworking hours in those early married

days by going dancing in several of the available venues, and on weekends, they visited with Patti's grandmother in Seymour, occasionally making a perfunctory stop at her mother's place. Sometimes they visited Al's sister, and on many nights, they played board games and cards with friends. Most of their friends preferred spending those evenings at the Penny house—even though many lived in larger places. She and Al came to sense a certain magnetism that drew people to them, undergirding their already contented marriage, notwithstanding the day-to-day financial struggles.

Patti said, "In those days, our entire existence and thought process was about money and how we could get ahead in life." Perhaps that wasn't the most satisfying and psychologically pleasing manner to engage life, but it sustained them well enough.

7

Staying Strong

THE ONE-BEDROOM HOUSE ON NICHOLS suited their needs, but they were always planning by socking away what little money they could spare, always running thin with cash on hand, often to Patti's dismay. She dreamed of what grand things might lie ahead, but certain events periodically arrived to impede even the best-laid plans. And such a happy moment struck them in the late fall of 1961 and did not come entirely unbidden, causing them to bemoan their cramped one-bedroom quarters.

Patti's pregnancy set in motion the need for a larger house with a bedroom for the forthcoming baby. Such things as building a new house didn't happen immediately for the young couple. How could it? But with what they had saved in such a short time—and since they had already paid off Al's father for the earlier loan—they began ferreting away what little they could to build a house with two bedrooms, next door to their one-bedroom place. Eventually, the new house would turn into an actual home. A family home. And while that imagined new house pleasingly lay in their minds, the most important event of their marriage was about to happen; the birth of their first child would occur sometime in July, they were told. However, it would not happen before celebrating July 4, 1962. Who wants to sit at home on Independence Day, waiting for a baby to be born?

They invited the Seymour relatives—step-grandfather Ed, Grandmother, Mother, Dad, Paul, and Kenny—for a day at Doling Park. Patti and Al provided food and drink for a picnic lunch, which Patti prepared joyfully, even though she took her time, sitting down for brief rests. When would this child arrive?

Off they went to north Springfield, but as they approached the park, Patti thought all of Springfield must have had the same idea. Where would they park?

"This is as close as we're going to get," Al said. He waved to the rest of the family in the car behind them.

Patti said, "But the park's way up there."

"I'll carry the basket," he said. "You carry that baby."

But she wasn't at all sure. Whoever heard of a baby being born under exploding fireworks?

Al handed the picnic basket over to Ed and took Patti's arm. Surprisingly, they found a table, Grandmother spread a checked tablecloth on it, and everyone insisted that Patti sit. She would go for that.

After the food and fireworks, the walk back to the car was easier. The Seymour folks left, and immediately after getting home, Patti went to bed.

The next day was the finest of their young married lives. On July 5, 1962, Paula was born, bringing joy to Patti and Al—and to the entire Seymour family and Patti's large group of friends there.

———

Just two months later, a Seymour tragedy ensued when Ed Anderson, in a drunken rage, set his and Grandmother's farmhouse on fire by pouring kerosene from the kitchen to Patti's old bedroom. A neighbor passing by saw it and promptly extinguished it with a garden hose. There was no big flame, but smoke damage ruined the entire house.

A blessing in disguise? Perhaps it was because that was the end for Grandmother with Ed, an ending much to be desired. She never returned, and during her divorce proceedings, she came to live with Patti and Al because Patti's mother in Seymour refused to take her in.

Today, Patti says, "That was just another episode in a long list for which I had trouble forgiving my mother."

After the divorce settlement, Grandmother had enough money to buy a small two-bedroom house in Seymour. Patti said, "It was her castle. She was at peace."

Through sheer gumption, frugality, and perhaps stubbornness, Patti and Al finished their larger house in the spring of 1963. Paula had her own bedroom. They traveled to Buffalo, Missouri, and at Chapman's Furniture, they bought a few new pieces of furniture, all in the contemporary style: orange sectional, dining table, and bar stools.

And for added financial security, why not rent out their house next door? It made perfect sense. They were making a small amount of money from helping with Al's father's calves, and the rental income would help even more.

Thus, the next several months kept them busy: caring for their first child, continuing their jobs, the calf responsibilities, and the new business venture of renting the old house immediately after moving into the new one. They wanted their rental house to be right in every way. In each spare moment—and even when Patti felt Al should devote time to just the two of them—he made minor repairs they had put off and even added design features the new tenants would like. It was still their house, and they came to see it as one of their first major financial assets. Real estate, they were told, would always gain in value. It was hard to go wrong there.

In their new venture, they employed their strongest qualities: neatness, pride in ownership, and investing for the future. These were fine times in which they, at last, worked in tangible ways to design and craft a blueprint tailored by their own making.

Patti wanted to dive into a task that she had not yet mustered the time and effort to accomplish: refinishing the hardwood floors of their rental house. Instead, she and Al hired a person who made the floors shine. Surely renters would leap at the chance to rent. She and Al would be the best of landlords (a term Patti did not like since she was a lady, not a lord!) and would assiduously protect their proud investment.

They posted ads in both Springfield papers and three small towns in the area. They were selective when prospective tenants called and when a few of them arrived after hearing of the monthly rent. Patti gave the tour and sized up the people, gauging their ability to pay, social demeanor, and likelihood of keeping the house in good shape. She was an astute judge of character, and a developing business sense lurked under her bright countenance. That attribute followed her throughout the years, revealing itself when further business opportunities arrived.

One evening, after showing the rental property, she said, "I think I've found the people."

"What makes you think so?"

"They're young and both have good jobs."

"Where."

"She's a beginning cashier at Heer's, and he works at Frisco."

"Know how much they make?"

"No." She paused and said, "That's not a question I'd ever ask someone."

For all of Al's quiet assurance, which some people thought bordered on gruffness, Patti sensed she had won him over.

"Whatever you think," he finally said.

The next day, when she called them, they accepted immediately. She said, "First and last month's rent in advance."

Within a week, on a Saturday, Patti and Al watched from their living room window as the couple unloaded their possessions with the help of other people. Patti could not help but think of those hardwood floors, knowing property owners do not intrude unless under dire circumstance.

After the young woman returned from work in their one car, she often visited with Patti on the Penny small porch until her husband came home, always being picked up and returned by someone else. When she saw her husband arrive, the young woman scurried off, sometimes Patti thought a bit too quickly.

The evening visits continued, but each time, the woman appeared more somber than the last.

"Are you okay?" Patti asked.

"Oh, yes."

One night around midnight, Patti and Al awakened to loud voices next door, laced with what sounded like curses. The same disturbances happened regularly—late at night and always with angry shouting—but each morning, Patti and Al watched the husband leave. The two appeared none the worse for wear, considering the nights' activities.

The young woman's porch visits continued, and Patti finally mentioned the nightly commotion.

"Everything is all right," the woman said.

Patti knew better. "If there's ever a problem," she said quietly, "you can let us know. Al and I are always here."

The woman only stared into the distance.

How should Patti and Al face the problems next door? Do they intervene during one of their neighbors' nightly rows? Do they summon the police? Maybe, just maybe, the couple's disputes would die down. They might be going through what Patti's grandmother always referred to as "a rough patch." Didn't most marriages encounter difficulties at times? But the more Patti and Al discussed it, the more they could not relate to or understand such interaction within a marriage. Sure, they didn't always agree, but those disagreements never devolved into shouting matches. Could people who were actually in love—as Patti and Al were— resort to such violent verbal melees? And, most of all, Patti wondered if the violence was only verbal.

A few days later, Patti and Al noticed the couple's car remained at the house after the time when the woman usually left. Probably home sick.

When Patti returned from work and waited on the porch for the woman's daily visit, she did not show up. Not wishing to intrude and become the prying landlady, Patti hesitated to go over. She finally knocked on the door, considering it a visit from a friend and not the property owner.

On the third knock, the woman pulled a window curtain back slightly and opened the door a crack.

"Are you ill?"

"You could say that."

"What can Al and I do for you?"

"Oh, Patti." She flung the door open. Her hair was uncombed, and her left eye was swollen and red with a tinge of purple. "Look." She held up her left hand, and her wrist was twice its normal size. "I think he broke it."

"I'm taking you to the hospital."

"Wait here." She went back into the house, leaving the door open, and returned jangling her car keys. She wanted Patti to drive her to the hospital in her car, and after being treated, she would drive, if she could, to a friend's place where her husband didn't know about. "Could you get Al to pick you up at the hospital?"

Patti was amazed that the woman had devised such a solid

plan, which was carefully designed to keep her safe and not implicate Patti and Al. For the next week, the husband stayed home alone. Then he gave Patti and Al his notice of leaving, and they accepted with no questions asked.

When Patti and Al entered the house after the man moved, the wooden floors were still shiny, and there was not a bit of damage anywhere. To this day, Patti often thinks of the woman and hopes she remained safe.

She and Al placed another ad in the papers, seeking a second renter. This time, an older couple moved in and said they were happy to find such a fine house.

The man walked with a cane and was rather frail.

Patti later said to Al, using her darkest humor, "Doesn't look like there will be any assaults this time."

The retired couple paid their first and last month's rent, and the second month was paid on time. They were rarely outside the house—except for the wife occasionally leaving and returning with groceries—causing Al and Patti largely to ignore them and, on occasion, forget they even had renters. There was certainly no late-night shouting.

One evening, the woman showed up in tears. She said she was taking her husband to the hospital. He had been diagnosed with cancer the previous year and needed to see his doctor. "He's not getting any better."

"Are you taking him now?" Al asked.

"Yes. Could you help me get him to our car?"

"Certainly." He turned to Patti, who was behind him listening.

They walked with the woman to the house, and the man was standing in the doorway, looking frailer than the first time they saw him. Patti and Al at once smelled something, and it wasn't floor varnish. Dogs were scampering through the house. The place looked like it had never been cleaned.

Patti, without asking, stepped quickly through the door. Her bright, shiny floors were spotted with stains. She knew they were caused by dog urine. Al moved in behind her and counted eight small dogs. Patti and Al had never considered a pet policy.

"My God," Patti said.

Al closed the door, and they walked outside behind the couple. Patti stood on one side of the man with Al on the other side, keeping him upright and eventually into their car.

"Are you okay to drive?" Al asked the woman.

"We'll be just fine now," she said.

Patti and Al knew nothing about eviction, how it worked, or any procedures to set it in motion. The man was obviously dying. Could they tell them to leave with him in that condition? He lived six months, mostly in the hospital, before dying. Then they evicted the woman, and the sheriff forced the issue. He said he had never seen a house in such ruin. The woman took the dogs with her. Al and Patti were left with the cleanup, thus ending their business venture into rental properties. Never again. They sold the rental house and property to L. D. and Helen Smith, and they became neighbors *and* friends.

Patti and Al had learned a sad sign-of-the-times employment fact when she became pregnant with Paula. Lily Tulip's rigid policy forced pregnant employees to leave without pay when four months pregnant—or "when you are showing."

Patti raged within herself at this indignity, and she voiced her concern to management—to no avail. Later in her career, she remembered this unfairness and implemented fair and just workplace policies at Penmac.

Four weeks after Paula was born, Patti returned to Lily Tulip in Production Planning and stayed until learning of her second pregnancy. John was born October 9, 1964, another joyful arrival. However, she also faced, again, the forced leave policy. This time, she did more than rage. She filed for unemployment benefits, an almost unheard of move in those day, but the personnel (today it is called human resources) director, a female, supported her case. Patti won.

She decided to stay at home with her children for a while, and when John was two years old, she sought a job back at Lily Tulip—but was told none were available. (Did management recall her unemployment benefit victory?) She scurried over to Litton Industries and worked in Accounts Receivable for two years. And then, wonder of wonders, Lily Tulip called and wanted her to work in the Personnel Department. The business was flourishing and hiring, and applicants were lined down the sidewalk. She screened applicants and loved all aspects of her job. This would become the basis for her fascination and competence in hiring people to suit their skills with Penmac.

On November 22, 1963, news spread fast about John F. Kennedy's assassination. Patti walked into the large room where she worked.

Bill Bland, a black custodian, was emptying a wastebasket. "Patti, what's all the commotion about?"

"Oh, Bill, our president has been shot."

He looked at her, immobile, appearing unable to speak. He left for a while and then came back and said, "Patti, I knew you weren't one of those who would say such a thing to be hurtful when the president was such a friend to us."

Patti was solidly aware of the covert and sometimes overt racism throughout much of Lily Tulip and much of Springfield. All black employees at Lily Tulip held menial positions.

Bill said, "You've always treated me and all the others very well. And we're grateful."

"Thank you, Bill." She had been unaware that he thought of her that way.

Today, she says, "I didn't like the mistreatment of the black employees—even though that was the culture of the time. Many of the injustices we are now facing are because of the strong feelings in our community that minorities and women are inferior."

Later, when she was working hard to shepherd the fledgling Penmac into existence and into some kind of viability, she said, "I quickly learned when I was out 'selling' Penmac to play the Scarlett O'Hara role. It worked, but I didn't necessarily like it. Not only did the men I called on give me business, but some became my mentors. I never challenged their authority."

Strong businesswomen such as Patti did what they could to foster gender equality and help promote opportunities for all people in the workplace.

8

What Now?

AS THE 1960S SPED BY, Patti still worked, but her devotion to her children took precedence. She steadfastly provided the best experiences and activities for them, but one occurrence remains indelibly inscribed in Patti's memory. She worked at Litton Industries, and the management adhered to strict on-time attendance, a policy she accepted gladly. However, she might have broken and/or cursed that guideline one particular time: the day Paula started kindergarten.

Timing would mean everything. If all went well, especially if the bus arrived early, Patti could wait with Paula at the bus stop and watch her climb aboard and perhaps wave goodbye as the bus rumbled off on that first day. Wasn't that a parental rite of passage? Even for a working mother? Other mothers were standing at the stop with their children, but none of them—besides Patti—were looking at their watches. Her work at Litton Industries was going well, and she mostly understood the pressure management placed on employees. Many had violated the on-time policy, something she was ambivalent about, especially on this day. Standing there, she spoke briefly with two mothers, said goodbye to Paula, got in her car, and waved to her daughter waiting in her blue-checked dress, holding her new lunch box. Patti said, "I cried all the way to work."

She was performing the dual roles of working and rearing children, and in that instant, she was succumbing to the pressure of the workplace. She wondered why only *one* parent should bear so much of both responsibilities; the question haunted her for years. Always in her working life—before and after starting Penmac—she advocated for fair and equal workplace opportunities for women. American cultural standards and customs forced women to bear the greater role of parenting.

In 1966, Patti and Al built a new house and bought five acres on Weaver Road, and they still live there. Patti's longtime friend Carol Scott and her husband, Ronnie, bought a house next door. John was two years old then. He and Barry Scott—Carol and Ronnie's son—became best friends, mostly exploring and playing outside, including using scrap lumber they found from the home building sites close to them to construct a tree house.

Nothing topped an early memorable event of John's young life—one Patti and Al recall vividly—when he and Barry were playing in their basement.

"What are you two doing down there?" Patti yelled.

"Playing cowboy," both yelled.

Too quickly, Patti thought.

After thirty minutes, things became quiet—none of the clamorous roughhousing she was used to hearing.

"Boys?"

Nothing.

"John?"

Nothing.

She went down. *What is that smell?*

The two glassy-eyed boys sat with their backs against a wall.

Before them were two open bottles of liquor. One bourbon, one scotch, Patti recalls clearly. The two cowboys had raided the well-stocked basement bar and were playing saloon. After John vomited, Barry's mother rushed her son to the ER, but all turned out well.

Patti said of John, "He was an aggressive boy and had definite ideas about what he would or would not do."

According to Patti, "The 1970s were an extremely busy time of my life. I was working part-time at Lily Tulip, was PTA president, Cub Scout leader, and Camp Fire Girls leader." Under Patti's tutelage, the Cub Scout troop formed baseball and basketball teams, and Patti applied her leadership and organizational skills from her activist days in Seymour.

She watched her grandmother's health decline and assumed the usual aging processes were in play. But on New Year's Eve 1971, Patti learned from her grandmother's doctor that she was terminally ill with cancer. The news landed heavily with Patti. "I was beside myself." This was the woman who allowed Patti to stay after leaving her mother and bicycling to her house; the woman whom Patti considered more her mother than her own mother; a sheltering arm through elementary and high school; the woman who did without niceties for herself so Patti could be outfitted in stylish clothes; the woman who had tolerated an alcoholic husband, Ed, and essentially nurtured him through those difficult drunken days.

Patti was in Springfield, and Grandmother was in Seymour, which did not afford the best circumstance and was certainly not the most convenient for Patti. In addition to navigating her grandmother's ship, she knew she must continue working and volunteering for her children's activities. Grandmother could not help herself.

Patti reluctantly surveyed nursing homes close to Seymour and might have landed a good one for her grandmother, but she "decided there was no way I could do that. Grandmother wanted to be in her home." Then came the most surprising news from California: Patti's mother would come to Seymour to care for Grandmother during the day. And Ed agreed—and wanted—to stay at night. Patti said, "Ed would never give up hope that she wasn't going to get well," but others knew differently.

Patti went to Seymour every day, bathing her, and trying to buy and prepare food she could eat. The community rallied by bringing flowers from their gardens, often wildflowers they had picked expressly for her, and Grandmother cherished them. The flowers brought her much delight.

She died peacefully on June 4, 1972. Patti recalls how Grandmother obsessively feared debt throughout her life. Her last words to Patti were "Be sure all the bills are paid."

"This was the saddest time of my life," Patti said. "I still miss her. I can't talk about it today without tearing up."

Even though Grandmother and Ed were divorced, his life was never the same after her death. Patti says he was strong and helpful when sober and that she always wished for his addiction to cease, and she often thought it might, but his drinking worsened after Grandmother's passing.

Over the years, Ed had gone through one treatment program after another—with the same results. For a time, he lived with Patti and Al, finding work in a Springfield established restaurant, the Shady Inn, where he washed dishes. He did occasional farm work and moved back to his house in Seymour. Patti would travel to buy him food, just as she had done with Grandmother, but her tasks became increasingly difficult as he wasted away with pancreatitis.

One day, Patti found him crying on his back porch. "What's wrong."

He looked as sad as she had ever seen him.

"Ed, what's wrong?"

"My dog got hit in the road."

"Is he okay?"

"He died."

Just a year before, a drunk driver had hit Ed while he was driving his tractor. Patti had arranged to have him flown to the Veteran's Administration Hospital in Columbia, Missouri, for treatment, and he barely escaped death. Now he was grieving the death of his dog on his back porch.

A week later, he died. Patti said, "After all his anguish from alcoholism and pancreatitis, he died a terrible death." Patti cared for him throughout his suffering.

The 1970s were eventful in many ways. Soon after Grandmother's death, Al received a large promotion at Hoerner, and the stock in which he had so faithfully invested split. However, the new corporate management was unacceptable to local management in Springfield, and the general manager, plant manager, and sales manager all resigned and formed their own company: Southern Missouri Containers. The company was sold again to Champion International and then again to Stone Container. Al remained throughout the changes, which proved beneficial, but his stress mounted in his managerial positions.

Patti continued working and rode out the 1970s as wife, parent, and company employee, but changes were in the offing. Those changes would bring many rewards and challenges.

Paula's sixteenth birthday, July 5, 1978, brought more than the usual happy wishes. It also heralded her freedom to obtain a driver's license and transport Paula and John to and from school activities. Patti was still part-time at Lily Tulip, and the notion of freedom that had struck Paula with her driver's license also hit Patti almost like an epiphany: The kids weren't completely reared, but she no longer needed to deliver them back and forth from their various goings-on. Hadn't she taken the part-time job at Lily Tulip to rear children? Perhaps she should now go full-time.

Much to her chagrin and surprise, when she inquired about full-time positions there, none were available. The immediate shock soon left. Wasn't she still the Patti from Seymour who forever searched for new experiences and was always determined to make things happen on her own—with no disappointment too great to hold her down? Each day's newspaper ran myriad classified ads, apparently for anyone willing to put forth the gumption to call. She circled an ad or two and called, willing to sell herself on the phone then and there, but she was usually told to leave her number and "we'll get back to you." She soon learned she wasn't the only person looking for work.

She had not circled a job opening at St. John's Hospital for a full-time personnel clerk, wondering if she lacked the skills the large hospital required. What did she know about hospital workers? However, she told herself, she already worked in a large firm at Lily Tulip, was a quick learner, and met people well. She called and had a short interview on the phone before being asked to interview in person. She learned the hospital was beginning what they termed a "fast growth mission."

Patti did not stop calling other places, and a few days after the interview she received a call. The full-time job was hers. This job became the launching pad later when she struck out on her own. She made a name for herself at St. John's, impressed those around her, and gained skills she would carry into the future.

The position in the Personnel Department offered her a unique opportunity to meet people and describe the skills that each position required before sending them on to an official interviewer. Everyone in the department took quick note of Patti's decorous comportment and innate ability to interact positively with all manner of applicants. She was soon offered an interviewer's position, and she gladly accepted.

However, nothing at Lily Tulip or her new entry-level St. John's position could have prepared her for the hard work and long hours. She was responsible for filling positions in all areas of the St. John's workforce—except for doctors, LPNs, and RNs. The bump in pay was indeed worthwhile, and the experience was invaluable for when, much later, she would start Penmac. She was also handed the duty of calculating benefits for retirees. How could she handle all those responsibilities? She went home each night more tired from work than any job she'd ever had. Al, Paula, and John surely noticed. She wanted to act at home with her usual zip, but all she desired was to put her feet up.

Al, as usual, gave comforting solace and offered practical advice. She should have all the time she needed on evenings at home to plow through the applicants she couldn't cover at work and set appointments since her receptionist did not have the time. Also, because of the hectic pace and commotion at work, she went to her office on most Sunday afternoons to calculate retiree benefits. Was she burdened by all the work? She was. Was it worth what she was going through? She was not sure. She needed help.

Since she was in charge of the bulk of St. John's hiring, she chose Jan Kinney. "She was the only person I could ever trust to screen applicants. She relieved me of the burden." Much later, after Patti was operating Penmac, she said she "went on the hunt for Jan. She came to work for me in May of 1989, and much of Penmac's success is because of her efforts."

Hospital recruiting continued apace. St. John's grew rapidly, and much of it was because of Patti's creative thinking and entering the Springfield community with innovative ideas. She slowly developed a close relationship with high schools, especially with advisers in charge of placing students in community workforce positions as part of their school curriculum.

Patti hired many Springfield young people to work at St. John's as attendants and dietary personnel. These entry-level positions gave them valuable real-world experiences. Patti also worked closely with the hospital's Training and Education Department in beginning a two-week nursing assistant program to offer a brief introduction to those who might consider a medical career.

Her most famous hire, the young Springfield native Brad Pitt, worked throughout his senior year in the Dish Room. A short time ago, he was back in Springfield—people over the years talk about and revere all the "Brad Pitt sightings" in town—to tour the hospital, and he shared his positive experience with the administration.

Patti established a reputation among employees as someone who listened with empathy, allowing them to speak of workplace problems and frustrations in private. She had no authority to act upon their issues, but her easy manner and honest listening skills helped many through difficult situations. Besides hiring them, she also nurtured many.

As time progressed, Patti also assumed the duty of handling promotions within the hospital. She was already encumbered with enough to keep her working some weekends, but she found the duty rewarding.

Jon Swope, who eventually became the president of the Mercy Health Systems, received his first promotion soon after Patti hired the eighteen-year-old as a hospital attendant ("runner") in the Physical Therapy Department. Another position opened in the department, secretary, and he applied. Among other qualifications, the position required that the applicant type forty words per minute. Jon tried and tried to meet that goal, but he failed every time. Eventually, Patti looked the other way and passed him. She said, "Over the years, he never forgot that, giving us plenty of laughs."

Yet, all was not perfect. The majority of the St. John's

workforce was female, which any employee or patient, for that matter, could detect. Since Patti hired most of the staff, she was keenly aware of the employee gender makeup. The hospital maintained a strict attendance policy—as Lily Tulip did—about which she had no quarrel, but she rose up in indignation after learning that females were penalized when absent to care for sick children. She had encountered the same type of discrimination at her previous employment, but the St. John's situation rankled her even more. She approached her boss, and the strict policy was softened. The administrators promised to take a closer look at each situation. Patti was pleased, but she knew the action was not strong enough.

As the 1980s swept in, Patti continued at St. John's. Al's work positions flourished, and he continued saving and investing. Paula married after high school, and in August 1983, she graduated from the University of Missouri-Columbia, majoring in fashion merchandising. She has three sons: Stu, Paden, and Cy.

John was an outstanding high school football running back. According to Patti, "His aggressive nature served him well on the football field." His prowess drew the attention of several big-name college programs, but during his senior year, he sustained a season-ending knee injury. He later graduated from William Jewell College with majors in business and public relations.

Patti's mother and her husband divorced in 1985, and Mary moved from California back to Springfield, becoming dependent upon Patti's long-suffering kindness toward her and her monetary support. In keeping with such generosity, Patti found Mary a house and five acres on Plainview Road, close to Patti and Al. Being comfortably situated, Mary needed to obtain a driver's license; she had never driven, even while living in Seymour. Who would be the driving instructor? The child began teaching the parent. While Patti's relationship with her mother had always been strained—to say the least—becoming the patient teacher was stressful, if not taxing, and fraught with the fear of car crashes at every turn. The instructor was fully up to the task, but the student could (or would) not learn. She failed every driving test she took.

So with Mary's indomitable spirit and independence, she would strike out walking on Plainview Road, a two-lane farm road, with cars whizzing by within inches of her. Patti was fearful for her mother's life and angry at Mary's brazen disregard for common safety. If that was not enough, Mary would happily and naively accept rides with anyone stopping to pick her up.

Mary began dating a cousin from Kentucky who had bought her several expensive diamond rings. She was always influenced by flashy fashion and susceptible to men's material advances. The cousin-boyfriend died in Prescott, Arizona, where they had been living. Mary had spent nearly all of his money, and his daughter had to finance the funeral and burial. Mary's mental state deteriorated. Patti said, "She went a little crazy," and Patti eventually received power of attorney over her mother. Patti said, "It was a big mess."

As Patti's work at the hospital increased, she felt she could not advance without a college degree. After much deliberation, she enrolled at Southwest Missouri State, which she had attended for one semester. She says, "I just didn't have the persistence. It took every minute of what little time I had." She dropped out, but other opportunities lay ahead.

Her community contacts continued, especially those within the Springfield Public Schools where she had volunteered during her children's years there. From kindergarten through high school, she tirelessly assumed leadership and came into contact with many teachers and administrators. Never the complaining parent, but always the supportive one, she impressed many by quickly learning the ins and outs of the educational system. She also saw the unmet needs and realized many educators were frustrated and felt helpless in operating within the system's faults. She empathized, but there was nothing she could do.

In 1984, several teachers asked her to run for the school board. She was humbled and honored, but she was also aware of her busy—and often hectic—schedule. Her supervisor at St. John's was in favor of her running for election. She needed four thousand petition signatures to run, which she got, with many St. John's employees helping collect the signatures. She ran unopposed.

Everything didn't exactly come up roses after winning the election. The St. John's administration balked about her spending work time on school board matters, which was nearly impossible not to do with the luncheons, spur-of-the-moment meetings, and occasional school visits. The supervisor who had heartily endorsed her running had new responsibilities, and the new one did not take kindly to Patti's school board duties. On the surface, Patti understood why someone might object, but she more than compensated for any lost time at her desk by working double-time. Anyone at the hospital who knew Patti and her work ethic fully vouched for her time, loyalty, dedication, and resultant production.

A new supervisor hit the scene whom Patti described as "a spoiled brat." She says, "To say the new supervisor and I didn't click was an understatement." When her annual review rolled around, he gave her a poor one. "I still have that review," Patti says today. He accused her of favoritism in hiring, insubordination, and a few other infractions. Patti spent the next weekend gathering evidence rebutting his comments. She submitted her written case to her supervisor's supervisor, and the document worked its way to the top administrator, Allen Shockley. Patti won the appeal, and all the untrue comments were removed. Word traveled rapidly through the system, and people admired Patti for standing up for herself. She continued on the school board, worked overtime at St. John's, and compensated for any time missed.

She brought to the school district the keen organizational skills she had learned and fostered in Seymour and then each subsequent job. She established such functions as the R-12 Roundup, an extravaganza to celebrate each new school year, a skill she mastered by heading up and carrying out many St. John's picnics. If people doubted Patti's dedication and effectiveness in both her job and her school district endeavors, they were not paying close attention.

While on the school board, she met Jackie McKinsey, whom Patti said always came to the meetings highly prepared and organized, as opposed to Patti's personal admission she often "flew by the seat of my pants." Jackie had just lost her husband (a doctor at St. John's) to a tragic death, and she needed a job. Patti arranged for Jackie to interview for the recently available job of gift shop manager at St. Johns. Jackie was highly qualified, just recently receiving a degree from Southwest Missouri State, but she was not hired.

However, all was not lost for Jackie McKinsey—or Patti. The two considered opening a new enterprise. It might prove to be successful—or not—but some things might be worth a try.

9

Go for It

PATTI FELT GOOD ABOUT WINNING the appeal to amend her negative annual work review, and many employees applauded her forthrightness to advocate for herself. She was delighted to have the unfairness stricken from her record, but she could not allay the hurt feelings resulting from being falsely accused, especially in the light of what she and others knew of her work. Hadn't she accomplished all she could at St. John's and reached the pinnacle of what she might offer to the hospital? The work review fiasco, as her grandmother might say, "stuck in her craw," and while Patti should have put the ordeal behind her, she became restless and considered moving on to something else.

The notion of starting her own business took shape and would not turn her loose. Al planted the seed that would eventually blossom into her own business: providing temporary employees to businesses needing help. She resisted Al's suggestion at first, claiming she knew nothing about such things, until he reminded her that she had a full career of recruiting and hiring personnel at St. John's.

"Don't you know how that works?" he asked, gently probing.

At first, she thought he was joking. "Of course I do."

"Well ..." He gave her time to consider the simplicity and logic of his question.

"But ..."

He set her to thinking.

"You'd be good with your own business," he said. "Why don't you do what you know best? Hiring people."

And with that simple statement, he gave her his support. On their first date, Al told her he had always wanted to start his own business. Was this his way of fulfilling a dream?

"At my plant [Stone Container], we have a temporary work-force in the Labeling Department. They put labels on pizza boxes and save me lots of money in labor because their pay rate is lower than the regular employees."

"How many employees in that department?"

"Fifteen. I'll bring home an invoice and show you what I mean."

The next day, when looking at the invoice, she couldn't believe what she saw. "The employee is making *this*—and you are being billed *this*?"

In an instant, Patti recognized the chance to have a viable business with all the risks involved and the added competitiveness she always sought. She could not bear to lose at anything. A few years earlier, someone had bet her five hundred dollars that she couldn't quit smoking. She quit and won the bet.

It was too much to think about. "I don't really understand the invoice that much. You keep talking about worker's compensation and unemployment—"

"Let me talk to Lloyd Anderson, the general manager, and see if he could give you that business."

"Business?"

"The temporary employee business—at Stone Container."

"Hold on there, Trigger! I don't *have* a business."

In his usual manner, Al grinned and walked away. "Let me talk to him."

Al did, and Lloyd Anderson went to his district manager. Two days later, Al said, "It's set up. You can have the fifteen—if you want them—to get started."

"You really think I could do this? And make money?"

Patti met with Jackie McKinsey about being partners, and Jackie agreed. Patti said she would check into franchises and meet with Ruby Letsch, the owner of Kelly Services, a major staffing company. Ruby said Kelly Services had stopped using franchise offices, which Patti considered to be in her favor.

After doing some research, Patti liked Adia Services and how their promotional materials were thorough and professional. She requested a business plan from Adia, which she took to David Harrison, another school board member.

After only briefly perusing the plan, he said, "Patti, why in the world would you want to pay Adia 30 percent of your gross? You should start your own service. No one in Springfield knows who Adia is." He looked away. "But lots of people know Patti Penny."

And before the dust settled, she and Jackie borrowed sixteen thousand dollars from Empire Bank—all with Al's enthusiastic approval. Terry Brown, a CPA, and Don Duncan, an attorney, said they would help in any way, if needed. Patti tendered her month's notice at St. John's Hospital and felt relieved and happy.

It all took shape quickly, a private, non-franchise business run by two smart and savvy women with many close ties to Springfield, name recognition, and a good client already in the fold. Soon, they leased eight hundred square feet of office space in the new Cherrystone Building at Cherry and Glenstone streets.

Patti vividly recalls when she and Jackie were in the Ollis

and Company insurance office. A secretary answered the phone and said, "Patti, it's your husband. He'd like to speak with you."

She glanced at Jackie then answered.

"I have some news," Al said, his voice shaky, unlike him.

Was something wrong with one of their children? "What?"

"Lloyd Anderson just received a call from corporate headquarters. Your promised contract with Stone Container will not go through."

The phone in her hand must have weighed a hundred pounds. She couldn't speak.

"They say it would be a conflict of interest," he said.

"Whose interest, dammit?"

"I work for the company."

It couldn't be. Ron Gordon-Ross wouldn't go back on his word with something this important. She handed the phone back to the secretary, walked out without saying a word, and went directly to see Don Duncan. Her newly acquired attorney made several calls on Patti and Jackie's behalf, but the corporate offices would not budge. There was no legal recourse.

Looking back on that time, Patti says, "I was devastated—but held things together. I told Jackie she was certainly free to leave, but she stayed. We had no income and no way of paying the debt."

Who should arrive on the scene in rescue mode? Al Penny. Frugal Al. He said he had plenty of money saved. "Go for it," he said. And they did.

At the annual Stone Container Christmas party, the divisional manager, of all people, asked Patti to dance. While they danced, he said, "Patti, you will thank me someday."

For screwing me out of fifteen placements and going back on your word? She didn't know whether to vomit or punch him in the nose, but she did neither.

Patti Penny and Jackie McKinsey began Penmac, a fledgling business, hoping to secure enough clients to get things rolling. Jackie asked a friend to volunteer at the front desk and stayed at the office.

Patti hit the streets each day to find businesses that needed temporary help. Just one business would do for starters, and it seemed reasonable to check with St. John's Hospital. Patti's former employer needed a short-term secretary, but Penmac had no secretaries available. Patti called upon a friend, Cathy Burkett, the best secretary she knew, who had just retired from the Frisco Railroad. Cathy took the job, Penmac's first success, and stayed at St. John's for six months.

What happens if the bank holding your business loan has a fire and needs a cleanup crew immediately? If you're Patti, you call you son's high school football coach, and he sends several players to do the job.

Patti learned that a man who lost his job at Lily Tulip had started a food-preparation business, Irene's Quick Spuds, and needed employees immediately. Penmac got the order.

Al's company did business with Quinn Coffee Company, and one of its vendors contacted Patti when it needed temporary help in its spice department. Another order.

Patti's son, John, said his friend's father owned a company called Vinyl Moldings and could use some temporary workers. Another order.

While serving on the school board, Patti had met someone owning a plating company who needed help. Another order.

After a year, Penmac had thirteen clients and fifty thousand dollars in accounts receivable. Each month, Patti hand wrote paychecks using a chart for withholding.

The business grew. After making a cold call to Diversified Plastics in Nixa, Missouri, Patti received an order for thirty people. It was a fine client, but she needed a large "name" Springfield company, and after a cold call to Durkee French Foods—one of the premier employers in town—the human resources director said he would place an order if Penmac lowered its rates. And therein lay a problem.

When starting the business, Penmac's CPA built a rate sheet, and Patti and Jackie agreed not to go below 30 percent. Patti was willing to go lower, but Jackie wanted to keep the business small, thereby assuming little risk. Patti lowered the rate, thus ending the partnership. After all, the primary reason for owning a business was to be her own boss.

But how to divide and how to split? When beginning the business, John insisted on a buy/sell agreement. Patti offered Jackie half of the accounts receivable—and Patti would assume the debt. If Jackie did not take the offer, Patti decided she would open her own staffing company, Penny Personnel, and would not sign a non-compete agreement, making clear that Patti would stay in the staffing industry. Jackie agreed to the proposal. Patti says, "At the time, I never felt so exhilarated. It was like a millstone had been lifted from my neck. In July 1989, I was free."

The front desk secretary left because of the split, but a secretary Patti had placed at St. John's was available and came to work—along with another person Patti hired at St. John's to help screen applicants. "The two of them were so instrumental in getting the business growing. A friend of a friend did the payroll on her kitchen table, giving me the opportunity to go out daily selling our services."

Carol Fritts, Patti's best friend, helped her through those early times. Patti said, "She was a guiding light on many issues and was brilliant with the written word." In 1995, they started the Angel Company as a gift shop and retail business, losing forty-five thousand dollars in the first year. Patti gave the business to Carol, hoping she could make it successful, but it failed. Patti lost the best friend she ever had, and she would never enter into a partnership again. Ever. "I am not partner material," she says. "Except for Al."

What business does not go through hard times? Penmac was not immune to such downturns. For reasons Patti still does not know, one of the directors at the chamber of commerce did not care for her and encouraged a local couple to open a staffing franchise in Springfield to compete with Penmac. The female owner was elected the first female president of the chamber of commerce.

The chamber and the Tourism Department wanted to display snowflakes around town for Christmas decorations and asked Penmac to provide workers to assemble them. Based on Penmac's need for business, Patti sent crews for the work. Consequently, Penmac paid the workers and billed the business owner the chamber had hired. "I never received one dollar of the twenty-five thousand dollars I invested in the project. I really don't know how I survived except that the Lord was with me."

Patti called on General Electric many times, but the human resources director said he was locked in with Manpower. Finally, the director said Patti could send one person on a job for which there had been much turnover, and Penmac's person stayed for thirteen years. Gradually, the director hired Penmac for "casual workers" that Manpower would hire after ninety days. In 1992, the director said he would let Penmac bid on Manpower's full contract. Penmac won the low bid and received the contract in October.

In that same year, the Midwest—along the Missouri and Mississippi Rivers—experienced what is still considered an historical flood, wiping out thousands of HVAC systems. General Electric needed a significantly increased workforce and contracted Penmac for three hundred workers. Sterling Macer, the Springfield General Electric human resource manager, knowing Penmac needed the money, persuaded the corporate executives to pay weekly.

Patti says, "It was a wonderful relationship for many years until General Electric sold its motor business. Sterling Macer retired and came to work for me. He was my mentor and taught me so much about the corporate world—such as never to bid in whole numbers." Mr. Macer's guidance was exceedingly helpful.

While Penmac grew, the accounting functions did not keep up. "I desperately needed to hire a real chief financial officer. Leah Ann Iaguessa came on board. She had worked in public accounting and was an auditor for thirteen years. She began by building a team of qualified people to work in the department. She saved Penmac."

Penmac's growth required more and more managers. "I was so pleased to offer women an opportunity to be entrepreneurs like myself. God blessed me over and over to bring these hardworking, smart women to my doorstep. They believed in our mission." Patti worked closely with them as she went to their offices, collaborating and sharing ideas, all backed by the company's motto of "Placing People First."

"When I reflect on what was most important to me, it was the chance to help women. None had human relations experience. One was a hog farmer, one a daycare provider, one a state worker, one a stay-at-home mother, wife, and community activist. We have all been blessed beyond our greatest expectations."

10

Just Can't Sit Back

DOES SUCCESS ALWAYS BREED MORE success? If, for example, clients keep coming on board, does that mean halting all-out pushes each day as Patti operated in the infancy years? She pondered the risks of expanding, of eventually losing past gains by overextending resources, which could lead to diminishing returns. There was much to consider.

Meanwhile, finding workers to send out to clients was never a problem. Newspaper classified ads served Penmac well, and people came looking for temporary work: "I read about you in the paper," they would say. In the beginning, that was the prime means of bringing people into the office. Then word-of-mouth referrals from one satisfied worker to another potential worker kept the phones ringing—as well as referrals from one company to another.

Patti continued her many community activities, including boards and volunteer duties, and more and more people learned about Penmac. The business began garnering "lots of good press," she said. "We often made news," which, of course, brought nothing but positive reactions, eliciting more business.

Still, since business was doing so well, should she consider opening up new markets? Patti's former CPA, Terry Brown, was the CFO at The Underground and suggested she open an office in Carthage, Missouri, a thriving town west of Springfield. At first, she was reluctant.

"There's plenty of business there," he said.

"But in Carthage?"

He told her about The Underground, a firm that stored supplies and products in large caves. There was lots of truck traffic in and out, as well as forklifts moving inventory within, and it all required temporary workers. The caves were run by Americold, named for the cool temperatures within the caves, which were suitable for storing fresh items.

Brown suggested expanding there, and Patti opened Penmac's first office outside of Springfield. Penmac sent employees to Harry and David, a firm using fresh fruit for gift baskets. The cool caves assured the product would last longer than in other storage units. Patti hired Linda Kinney to manage the office. Soon after, another office opened in nearby Joplin, Missouri, which Kinney also managed. However, business declined in both places, through no fault of Penmac, as the local economies took a downturn.

Penmac clients General Electric and Emerson Electric needed workers in other states, leading to expansion outside Missouri. Current Penmac CEO Tim Massey says, "Penmac formed organic relationships in the local communities by hiring local managers, investing them with an entrepreneurial spirit to increase Penmac's influence and profitability." Patti did not like layers of management; she wanted to establish a ground-level approach instead of going through multiple layers. This flat organizational structure simplified matters.

Penmac spread widely in Missouri and in other states.

Missouri offices included Springfield, Ava, Branson, Camdenton, Carthage, Eldon, Houston, Joplin, Lamar, Lebanon, Lee's Summit, Marshfield, Monett, Owensville, Poplar Bluff, and West Plains. Other states with offices were Arkansas, Kansas, Mississippi, Minnesota, Oklahoma, South Carolina, Tennessee, and Virginia.

Today, Penmac retains some accounts it has served for thirty years. Long-standing clients help ensure profitability. In 2018, the company processed more than 28,000 W-2 tax forms, and each temporary worker filed a form.

Penmac continually faces challenges, and the company is always hindered by national economic downturns, especially in the manufacturing sector. For example, in 2008, an all-encompassing recession struck the country, and Penmac was heavily affected. Before 2008, the company did ninety million dollars' worth of business each year. After the recession, sales decreased to fifty million dollars per year. Tim Massey said, "In 2009, Penmac hit the ground running, and by 2014, sales increased to one hundred million dollars." In 2018, Penmac did one hundred thirty-three million in sales. There are nineteen thousand staffing firms in the United States, but only 150 are doing one hundred million dollars in sales per year. Penmac is a leader in revenue growth.

Many companies use an Employee Stock Ownership Program (ESOP) as a means to operate a business and allow employees to invest in the company. In 2010, Penmac instituted ESOP, which means the company is 100 percent owned by the employees. This includes a large portion of the temporary staff. Tim Massey says it has worked well. Penmac is the largest employee-owned staffing company in the United States, and out of all American companies, it is the second largest employee-owned firm.

Employees must wait one year to qualify for ESOP and can be fully vested, as of 2020, in six years and after they have worked a minimum of one thousand hours. The payout is usually at retirement age. Thus, through the ESOP structure, Penmac does not pay taxes; instead, it pays vested workers when they retire. How is the company able to make the payments and not hurt its cash flow? Penmac's CFO, Leah Ann Iaguessa, said, "The company must plan ahead for those cash payments." How can it plan ahead? "Opening new offices, maximizing profits, expanding wisely, and saving for the future." Currently, Penmac has thirty-two offices in nine states.

Before ESOP, Penmac was a family-owned Subchapter S corporation. While attending a national convention with other staffing companies present, Patti was asked to sell Penmac. She pondered the ramifications—and not positively. With another corporation taking over, many of Penmac's corporate staff would surely be replaced with the new company's people. She could not do that to *her* people. She remembered the early struggles and sometimes downright defeats in establishing the Penmac brand over the years, and the company eventually stood strong. She understood and greatly appreciated all the employees' loyalty and hard work, and she had established and nurtured the company mostly herself. Her overriding official stamp on the company had always been to treat people honestly and fairly. Would a new corporation do that?

The ESOP was an enticing option. The management structure would not change, and Patti's family would remain on the board of directors, keeping the Penmac brand intact, with the continued opportunities of expanding, just as the company always had. ESOP's benefits far outweighed its downsides, and it fit well with the overall business model Patti had established years before: Always open up new markets. "We just can't sit back," she says. That hallmark notion that drove her in Seymour still drives her today.

Penmac's corporate team acknowledges Patti's leadership and appreciates the company's history and how Patti's unflinching dedication brought the company to its present state. When Leah Ann Iaguessa began with Penmac in 1997, she had Patti's full trust and backing to shore up the financial system. Iaguessa says, "Straightening up the accounting procedure was a challenge. It needed efficiency." Not many executives would entrust such freedom to a CFO, but Patti did.

When asked to describe Patti's personality as the company's head, Iaguessa said, "She has the perfect entrepreneurial spirit. She is hands-on and does not procrastinate about anything. She focuses on serving the customers, staying flexible, and tailoring to their needs. Patti has helped many people, especially getting women into management positions."

Iaguessa's most telling comment: "Patti takes it upon herself to allow others to help themselves." Patti values hard work and does not require of others what she would not do herself.

In Penmac's early struggling years, when workers did not have transportation, she spent much time picking them up at their homes and driving them to their work sites for their shifts. Day or night, it did not matter to Patti. Today, Penmac vans help workers get to their jobs, and the workers pay nominal fees that are deducted from their pay.

Patti soon discovered many women workers did not have and could not afford appropriate clothes for professional and office jobs. One block from the Springfield Penmac corporate building is a space called Suit Yourself. Along with other businesswomen, Patti began donating women's professional clothing where Penmac temporary workers and other women referred by different organizations can choose suitable office wear, without paying, from a wide selection of styles and sizes. Penmac contributes cash and labor, and the entire business community noticed.

Word spread about Penmac, and honors and kudos soon

followed because of its founder's acute business sense, creativity, and abiding compassion.

————

Even before Penmac opened, while she was working at St. John's and serving on the Springfield School Board, Patti's audience widened. Groups asked her to speak to students, tell her story, and inspire others, especially young women. In 1985, she addressed a group of Springfield high school women about her struggles and successes:

"Women are no longer slaves as in early cultures. We have the freedom of choice. You, as young women, can choose to do anything you wish, and that includes housework. Also space exploration. Anything freely, consciously chosen. I made the choice to try to do it all. I wanted to be a homemaker and mother, I wanted a job, and I enjoyed being of service to others."

In the speech, she introduced the school district's newly formed Parents as Teachers, which involved parents playing a major role in their children's lives—at home and school. "I have a reverence for education. Being on the school board is an education. There isn't any school for board members. When you are elected, you must start learning. You talk to people in education, attend seminars and workshops. You have endless hours of reading so that you become an informed member. It is a commitment and a challenge."

She understood that many of the women in the audience did not agree with everything at the school, such as the attendance policy, but she said she would always try to provide every opportunity for students' learning. "A wasted mind is a tragedy our society cannot afford."

She added, "I've shared what has really been important to me: my family, a supportive and responsible husband, children who respect me, friends, the freedom to choose my own destiny, education, meaningful work, and giving of one's time and talents to make our world a better place. What I haven't told you is that my faith in God is the source of my strength to accomplish my many tasks."

Three years later, in 1987, while still employed at St. John's Hospital, she spoke at the fiftieth anniversary celebration of Cooperative Occupational Education (COE). The evening was dedicated to honoring employers who provided jobs for COE students. She said, "I much prefer to think that we are really here tonight to honor those students who successfully combine their academic work with the world of work. Many of our COE students [at St. John's Hospital] are presently pursuing careers in radiology, respiratory therapy, surgery, physical therapy, laboratory, print shop, dietary, and supply. Through the guidance of their COE counselors, students come to me prepared for their job interviews. They are conscious of their appearance, their application is neatly printed, and they have learned that good eye contact and positive answers are important ingredients to securing a job."

Patti vividly recalls when she learned how certain state policies negatively impacted her business. "At the beginning of Penmac, I wasn't paying much attention to worker's compensation or unemployment insurance. In 1993, my CPA discovered those two programs drained considerable revenue from Penmac. I hired a retired worker's compensation auditor to examine our files. He warned our worker's compensation claims were out of control. I was shocked to learn that within a short time, those claims could actually run me out of business."

Patti consulted with the Missouri Chamber of Commerce and the Associated Industries of Missouri, learning that most manufacturers experienced huge costs from fraudulent claims, resulting largely from laws set by the Missouri legislature. Never one to sit back, Patti aggressively lobbied legislators and was quickly invited to testify before the legislature. In 1994 after Penmac started, she received a call from Governor Carnahan's office, asking her to chair the Missouri Board of Workforce Development.

"I thought this was a mistake because I was a Republican and the governor a Democrat, but I accepted and served for nine years, a wonderful experience." The board's members were from labor, education, and business. Patti said she clashed with labor officials, but over time, they compromised, resulting in legislation helping businesses and also assisting workers with training and education that prepared them for available jobs. "Today," says Patti, "those programs have expanded to a level I never dreamed possible. I'm thankful for the many people still working to help citizens be productive."

Patti also began more carefully monitoring Unemployment Insurance claims. "We made every effort to offer those losing jobs a new opportunity. If we had nothing to offer, then of course they were eligible for unemployment insurance."

Honors and high-level positions continued in the 1980s. She was awarded an honorary life member of the Missouri PTA; elected president of the Missouri School Boards, Region 10; and elected chair of the Missouri Board of Workforce Development. And after Penmac's opening, the honors continued, and more and more people understood her business-operating mantra: "You just can't sit back."

As Penmac prospered and expanded, so did Patti's influence, especially her ability to inspire and lead others by example. It was no surprise that, combined with her business sense and inspirational drive, she was awarded an honorary doctorate in public affairs from Missouri State University in 2009. She viewed this award as both humbling and rewarding, considering that, years before, she had withdrawn from the university to make her way into a business career. She accepted the honor graciously, and MSU bestowed it upon her graciously. The honor was not for business success, but for public affairs, encompassing far more than establishing, expanding, and maintaining the area's local economy. Serving the public was always one of Patti's principal goals, and it was a well-deserved honor.

In 2010, Patti delivered the commencement speech, written by Mason Duchatschek, at Missouri State University-West Plains, a companion campus east of Springfield. She began, "I am honored to be with you today and am in awe of your accomplishment. I never graduated from college. However, last year, Missouri State University conferred on me an honorary doctorate in public affairs. I have never been more humbled."

She reminded the graduating class of the national economic downturn of the previous two years, but that staffing businesses, such as hers, were on the rise. *Newsweek* had boldly proclaimed, "America is back."

"Change, in my opinion, is a necessity. I am an optimist; I believe necessity is the mother of invention. Those that are willing to adapt can prosper—not in spite of trying times, but because of them. I believe this because my family and I have lived through trying times."

She recounted for the audience how in Seymour in the 1940s, following the Great Depression, her grandfather's bank closed, thrusting her family from prosperity to poverty overnight. Her single-parent mother, out of necessity, "did what she had to do" and opened a beauty shop to make ends meet. "My mother's shop was successful because she worked hard and used societal change to her advantage. She was willing to adapt, so she prospered—not in spite of trying times, but because of them."

Patti explained how she lived with her grandmother on a small dairy farm when she was nine years old. The solitude was nearly unbearable. "The library became my second home, and I read voraciously, learning from others' perspectives, leading to a lifetime of learning. I was willing to adapt, so I prospered—not in spite of trying times, but because of them."

She concluded her address with these words: "One book that inspired me and influenced my thinking was *Gone with the Wind*. Scarlett O'Hara was my heroine. Her way of life was disintegrating, but she refused to be destroyed like her city was destroyed. Her defining moment was when she vowed, 'As God is my witness, I will never be hungry again.' She seized the opportunity to do something that was unthinkable for a Southern woman—she started her own business selling lumber to rebuild Atlanta. Scarlett was willing to adapt, so she prospered—not in spite of trying times, but because of them."

Patti's reputation as an entrepreneur and motivational speaker spread widely. In 2016, Tom Everett of the Elliot Robinson CPA firm invited Patti to speak at the Leadership Missouri Conference. She focused her remarks around seven points.

Faith. "I believe in answered prayers. If someone you love is at home when a burglar tries to break in and prays to God for help, God doesn't swoop down, grab the criminal by the scruff of his neck, and toss him into jail. The cops show up. The cops are the answer to prayer." She mentioned a sales manager who told some of his customers about Penmac, which opened up key doors for the company. Patti says he was an answered prayer.

Place people first. People, like a garden, need tending—whether they work for or with Penmac. "We work to teach them, inspire them, and nurture them for as long as it takes so they grow both personally and professionally."

Find a way. When employers in Ava, Missouri, said they needed workers with a high school education, and after the local school superintendent said he would not offer GED classes, Patti worked to offer those classes on site so the workers could qualify for jobs they otherwise would not have been able to get. Patti said, "We found a way or made one."

Entrepreneurial spirit. She said with information so readily available today, it's never been easier or faster to increase knowledge and gain experience that can dramatically reduce a traditional learning curve. "If you think you have an entrepreneurial spirit, start your day early before your regular job, then after the job, work for yourself until eleven or twelve at night." Such a spirit requires hours of dedication.

Trusted advisers. "When I hear people say they can't afford a CPA or lawyer, I scratch my head because my investments in expert advice generated much more in savings and new opportunities than I ever paid for them in the first place."

Service to others. "I love my family. I love my friends. And in many cases, I love my friends as if they were my family." Patti always invested her time and resources in serving others and supporting worthwhile causes. She has given freely to support libraries and the YMCA. "Healthy bodies and minds build healthy families and communities."

Gratitude, appreciation, and thankfulness. "When people perform well, they deserve respect and deserve to be recognized for their contributions. The words 'thank you' and 'I appreciate that,' regardless of whether expressed in words or deeds, are incredibly meaningful."

In 2017, Patti received one of the most locally coveted honors when the Springfield Chamber of Commerce named her Springfieldian of the Year. In her acceptance speech, she said, "The local business leaders, our employers, my family members, my church, the chamber of commerce, CPAs, lawyers, and other trusted advisers and friends have traveled this journey with me. I feel nothing but extreme gratitude and appreciation to each and every one."

Patti's true rewards, however, were not in the many honors

bestowed by others, but in the years of challenges and successes that eventually led many people to meaningful employment. It was all brought about by her honesty and dedication to helping others.

11

The Third Child

HEARING "YOU WILL NEVER MAKE it" from several people when starting her business could have been one of Patti's prime motivators, along with her already steadfast confidence, which harkened back to Seymour days when, as a high school freshman, she mustered the unheard-of notion that a senior trip to Miami Beach was within her class's reach.

Yet, thinking and doing don't often come wrapped in the same package or proceed in smooth tandem. Action does not always follow theory. Not many can have the vision followed by the wherewithal to bring about tangible results. Patti Penny might be a rarity, one of few visionaries who, through struggles and defeats, outlast the odds and others' disparaging attitudes.

But some obstacles were beyond her reach and her ability to make positive things happen. She could only stand by and watch alcoholism largely destroy her step-grandfather. She heard her beloved grandmother's sad admission: "Your grandfather went to bed with the bottle." Patti surely wanted to help rescue her step-grandfather and bring him to sobriety, but sometimes the best intentions hopelessly fail.

And not everything succeeded at Penmac. When in an effort to expand, Patti said, "I lost a million dollars trying to expand and grow my own. Some expansions just didn't make it."

The deteriorating relationship between Patti and her mother, Mary, finally reached a sad end, try as Patti might to steer her onto a steady course. After returning from California and divorcing Patti's stepfather, her obstinate mother lived close to Patti in Springfield. "She went through a bad time," said Patti. Mary insisted on wearing her large diamond ring because she always placed great importance on outward appearances, hoping to impress people.

Mary belligerently refused to buy a house in Springfield on a bus line—and she never learned to drive. Patti invoked power of attorney and sold the house and five acres on Plainview Road. Finally, in a furious snit, Mary bought a house in Springfield and went on what Patti called a "hunger strike," becoming abnormally thin, apparently out of spite.

Patti said, "I hired an angel, Mary Jo Burbee, to stay with Mom during the day, even after she was in a nursing home and until she died. Mom loved her." Patti's daughter, Paula, said Patti's mother was "out of place in Missouri and should have never come back from California. She didn't fit here and considered herself elite, wanting people waiting on her. She never lost the need for that."

Patti says, "I should have tried harder to have a relationship with Mom. One of my regrets."

Paula was married when Penmac started. "My mother considered Penmac her third child." As president of Penmac, Paula says she has "carried the torch" and "am somewhat driven like my mother. But since retiring and becoming chairwoman of the board, my mother has slowed down a lot. But if she doesn't like something, she will let you know."

When John was in college, he wrote an introspective autobiography for a class assignment:

> My mother is extremely complicated ... she was the disciplinarian of the household and the one I had to reckon with if I did something wrong ... she is the most loving, giving person I have ever known and gives more of herself to our family and friends than is ever expected ... she is made of iron ... my dad has never even yelled at me. I always felt his presence and unspoken discipline when I did something wrong ... I truly believe my parents enjoy fighting. It seems it makes their day to come home and let off steam at each other. But I honestly believe their relationship is made in heaven.

According to Patti, "John is now a valuable member of Penmac's board of directors. He has a better understanding of CEO Lean Ann Iaguessa's financial reports than the rest of us."

Penmac is indeed a family business. As Patti's "third child," she gives the company her care, nourishment, indulgent attention, and often discipline that any child needs and requires. A former employee who wants to remain anonymous said, "Patti expects a great deal from the company's employees and isn't afraid to let you know what she thinks. If you work there, you better be at your best at all times."

After Patti's retirement, in a Penmac promotional video celebrating its twenty-fifth anniversary, employees were asked to

describe her in one word or phrase: "ultimate entrepreneur ...
honest ... energetic ... down to earth ... inspirational ... work-
aholic ... creative ... strong-willed ... tenacious ... scary ...
problem solver ... stubborn ... likes to be in charge ... doesn't
understand the word *no* ... she *supposedly* retired." Most of those
descriptions could easily represent the qualities of a dedicated and
loving parent—or in Patti's case, the head of a thriving business.

Patti manifested an indomitable spirit and drive directed back
to Seymour, Missouri, her birthplace and home for her first seventeen years. In 1993, Blaine Childress offered a $350,000 matching
grant to Seymour for a new library. The community worked hard
to raise the money to match his grant, piquing Patti's interest.
"This was my first fundraising endeavor to help my hometown.
I loved it. The Friends of the Library started fundraising with
everything they could think of, and the money stalled. I started
helping and soon realized we probably wouldn't be able to raise
the money. Penmac had finally started showing a good profit, so
I donated $100,000 to help finish the project. It was my first real
'gift' to help the community. What a joy."

Seymour's Helen Lamb, historian and Seymour Museum
guide, proudly points to the town's YMCA and indoor pool that
serves the small town—thanks to Patti's persistent leadership and
fundraising. The Owen Theater, where the young Patti spent
many Saturday afternoons watching movies with her friends,
now stands fully operational as a place for public gatherings. It is
a symbol of Patti's generosity and willingness to give back to the
place of her formative childhood.

Penmac's operating slogan, "We place people first," carries
a dual meaning. When a company needs workers, Penmac must
be the first to offer the company qualified workers. Patti says,
"If we're not first to put someone in that job, our competitors
will." Secondly, and perhaps as important, Penmac must care for,
watch over, and nurture its own people—including meeting each

employee's needs as much as possible—since a business is only as good as its functioning employees. Call it team spirit or simply caring for each other, but the company *is* its people and not some amorphous entity.

Just as she has served others all her life, so should her business. As she is fond of saying, "You must be a servant." It is not just getting people into jobs; it is about truly caring about their well-being and hoping their lives progress successfully after leaving Penmac.

Her "third child" deserved as much support and rearing as each of her children. The parent and boss became the servant. What a way to live a life—and what a legacy.

About the Author

MICHAEL PULLEY earned a master's degree in literature from the University of Missouri-St. Louis. He's been published widely in literary journals and has written novels, a short story collection, a memoir, and bi-weekly newspaper columns. Pulley has been a high school teacher, college admissions counselor, college and university professor, and paralegal. He lives in Springfield, Missouri.

CPSIA information can be obtained
at www.ICGtesting.com
Printed in the USA
FSHW010651220420
69419FS

9 781480 886629